AF454304

NAVIGATING THE DATAVERSE

Taiwo Thomas

CONTENTS

FOREWORD

NAVIGATING THE DATAVERSE

In the modern world, data is more than just numbers, charts, and algorithms—it is the foundation upon which our societies, businesses, and innovations are built. From the way we communicate to the decisions that shape industries, data has become the most valuable currency of our time. Yet, as the Dataverse expands at an unprecedented rate, so too do the challenges of managing, securing, and ethically utilizing this vast ocean of information.

Navigating the Dataverse is more than a book; it is a guide to understanding the complex, dynamic, and ever-evolving landscape of data. It explores the key trends and technologies shaping the future, from artificial intelligence and machine learning to blockchain, quantum computing, and ethical data governance. More importantly, it asks the critical questions: How do we ensure that data serves humanity rather than exploits it? How do we balance innovation with responsibility? And how can businesses, governments, and individuals harness the power of data while safeguarding privacy, security, and ethical integrity?

This book is not just for data scientists and technologists; it is for business leaders, policymakers, educators, and anyone who seeks to understand the role of data in shaping our world. It provides a roadmap for those who wish to navigate the complexities of the digital age with confidence, insight, and foresight.

The future of the Dataverse is still being written. It is my hope that this book will empower its readers to not only understand data but to shape its impact in meaningful, ethical, and innovative ways. Whether you are a seasoned expert or just beginning your journey into the world of data, the insights within these pages will equip you with the knowledge and perspective needed to thrive in a data-driven future.

INTRODUCTION

We are living in the age of data. Every interaction, every transaction, and every decision we make whether online or offline generates data that fuels the modern world. From social media feeds and smart devices to financial markets and healthcare innovations, data has become the driving force behind technological advancements, business strategies, and societal transformations. It is the new oil, the new currency, and, some argue, the new power.

Yet, for all its influence, data remains a double-edged sword. While it offers opportunities for innovation, efficiency, and progress, it also presents challenges that demand urgent attention. Issues of privacy, security, misinformation, algorithmic bias, and ethical responsibility have sparked global debates about how data should be collected, used, and protected. Governments are scrambling to regulate it, businesses are competing to monetize it, and individuals are struggling to understand how it shapes their lives. In this fast-evolving landscape, one question becomes central: How do we navigate the Dataverse responsibly, effectively, and ethically?

This book is an exploration of that question. It delves into the technologies, trends, and transformations defining the world of data, from artificial intelligence and big data analytics to blockchain, cloud computing, and quantum advancements. It unpacks the opportunities and risks, the innovations and ethical dilemmas, and the ways in which data is redefining industries, governance, and human interactions.

More than just a guide to understanding data, *Navigating the Dataverse* is a call to action. It urges business leaders, policymakers, technologists, and everyday individuals to engage with data in a way that is informed, responsible, and forward-thinking. In the chapters that follow, we will explore how data is being harnessed to drive innovation, how emerging technologies are shaping its future, and how we can build a more ethical, secure, and inclusive digital world.

As we embark on this journey, one truth remains clear: The Dataverse is not just a technological phenomenon, it is a human one. How we choose to navigate it today will determine the future of industries, economies, and societies tomorrow. The challenge before us is not merely to keep up with the pace of change but to shape it in ways that benefit all. This book is your guide to doing just that.

CHAPTER ONE

INTRODUCTION TO THE DATAVERSE
UNDERSTANDING THE DATA UNIVERSE

In the digital age, the concept of the "Dataverse" has emerged as a critical framework for understanding the vast and complex universe of data that surrounds us. The Dataverse refers to the entirety of data that exists in the world, encompassing everything from structured databases to unstructured data streams, from personal information to global datasets. It is a universe constantly expanding, driven by the proliferation of digital technologies, the Internet of Things (IoT), and the increasing digitization of nearly every aspect of human life. The Dataverse is not just a collection of data points; it is a dynamic, interconnected ecosystem that reflects the complexities of the modern world.

The term "Dataverse" itself is a portmanteau of "data" and "universe," and it captures the idea that data is not just a resource but a vast, almost cosmic entity that we are only beginning to understand. Just as the universe contains galaxies, stars, and planets, the Dataverse contains datasets, data streams, and data repositories, each with its own unique characteristics and potential.

Understanding the Dataverse requires us to think beyond traditional data management and analysis and to consider the broader implications of data in our lives, our societies, and our future.

The Structure of the Dataverse

The Dataverse is not a monolithic entity; rather, it is a vast, multidimensional ecosystem composed of multiple layers, each with its own structure, function, and unique characteristics. Understanding its composition is essential for navigating the complexities of modern data science, artificial intelligence, and information management. At its core, the Dataverse is defined by how data is organized, stored, processed, and utilized. This structural complexity is what allows data to flow seamlessly across industries, drive innovation, and shape decision-making processes in an increasingly digital world. At the most fundamental level, the Dataverse can be divided into two primary categories: structured and unstructured data. Structured data refers to information that is organized in a predefined format, such as databases, spreadsheets, and tables. This type of data follows a consistent schema, making it easier to analyze, query, and process. For example, customer records in a retail database might include structured fields such as names, email addresses, purchase history, and transaction timestamps. Because structured data is highly organized, it is well-suited for traditional data processing and analytics tools, such as SQL-based databases and business intelligence software.

Unstructured data, on the other hand, consists of information that does not fit into a predefined format. It includes text documents, emails, images, videos, social media posts, audio recordings, and other forms of multimedia content. Unlike structured data, unstructured data lacks a fixed schema, making it more challenging to store and analyze. However, this type of data is incredibly valuable because it captures the richness of human communication, behavior, and interactions. For example, a company analyzing customer sentiment might need to process thousands of social media posts, product reviews, and customer service interactions—all of which contain unstructured data. With advancements in artificial intelligence and natural language processing (NLP), organizations are now able to extract insights from unstructured data in ways that were previously impossible.

Between these two categories lies semi-structured data, which blends elements of both structured and unstructured formats. This includes data stored in formats like JSON, XML, and YAML, where some level of organization exists but without the rigidity of traditional databases. Semi-structured data is commonly used in applications such as web services, API responses, and machine learning datasets, allowing for more flexible data storage while retaining a level of structured organization.

Domains of the Dataverse

Beyond the basic division of structured and unstructured data, the Dataverse can be further categorized into various domains based on ownership, purpose, and scale. These domains help us understand how data is generated, who controls it, and how it interacts with other datasets to create meaningful insights.

Personal Data

Personal data consist of information pertaining to individuals, including their identities, behaviors, and digital footprints. This includes personal details such as names, addresses, contact information, social security numbers, and biometric data. In the digital age, personal data has expanded to include online activities, browsing history, location data, and interactions on social media platforms.

With the increasing digitization of everyday life, personal data has become one of the most valuable assets in the Dataverse. Companies collect and analyze personal data to deliver targeted advertising, personalize user experiences, and improve customer service. However, privacy, data protection, and surveillance concerns have led to stringent regulations such as the General Data Protection Regulation (GDPR) in Europe and the California Consumer Privacy Act (CCPA) in the United States. These laws aim to give individuals more control over their data, ensuring transparency and ethical data practices.

Organizational Data

Organizational data refers to the information that companies, institutions, and businesses collect, store, and utilize to operate efficiently. This includes financial data, customer records, and employee information, sales metrics, operational analytics, and proprietary research. Organizations rely on data-driven strategies to optimize workflows, forecast market trends, and enhance decision-making.

For example, e-commerce companies analyze transactional data to identify purchasing patterns, predict customer preferences, and optimize inventory management. Similarly, banks and financial institutions use data analytics to detect fraudulent activities, assess credit risks, and improve investment strategies. With the rise of cloud computing and data lakes, organizations are now able to store vast amounts of structured and unstructured data in scalable environments, enabling real-time analytics and artificial intelligence applications.

Public Data

Public data includes information that is made available by governments, public institutions, and non-profit organizations for the benefit of society. This includes census records, weather reports, economic indicators, crime statistics, public health data, and transportation records. Public data is crucial for policymaking, scientific research, and social development.

For instance, meteorological agencies collect weather data from satellites and ground stations to provide accurate forecasts and track climate change. Governments release economic reports to inform businesses, investors, and policymakers about market trends and national productivity. Open data initiatives aim to make public data more accessible to researchers, developers, and the general public, fostering transparency and innovation. However, challenges such as data standardization, accuracy, and privacy concerns remain key issues in public data management.

Global Data

Global data encompasses large-scale datasets that reflect worldwide trends, economic activities, environmental changes, and social phenomena. These datasets are often aggregated from multiple sources, including international organizations, multinational corporations, and global research institutions. Examples of global data include climate change models, satellite imagery, population growth statistics, and international trade data.

An analysis of global data is essential for addressing global challenges such as climate change, public health crises, and economic stability. For instance, epidemiologists rely on global health data to track the spread of infectious diseases and develop containment strategies. Economies use international trade data to assess market fluctuations and predict economic downturns. As the world becomes increasingly interconnected, the ability to analyze and interpret global data will play a critical role in shaping future policies and innovations.

Interconnectivity Within the Dataverse

Each of these domains interacts with the others in complex and dynamic ways, creating a vast web of interconnected data. The boundaries between personal, organizational, public, and global data are often blurred as information flows freely across different sectors and applications.

For example, personal data can be aggregated and anonymized to create larger organizational datasets. A fitness app that tracks individual workout routines can use aggregated data to identify general health trends, which might then be shared with public health agencies to improve wellness initiatives. Public data, such as census reports, can be combined with organizational data to help businesses make informed decisions about market expansion and customer segmentation. Similarly, global data, such as satellite images of deforestation, can be used by environmental organizations to drive policy changes and corporate sustainability initiatives.

This interconnectivity underscores the importance of data governance, security, and ethical considerations. As data flows across different domains, it becomes crucial to ensure that it is used responsibly, remains accurate, and is protected from misuse. Organizations must implement robust data management practices, ensuring compliance with regulations while maximizing the value of the data they collect.

The Future of the Dataverse

As technology continues to evolve, the structure of the Dataverse will become even more intricate. The rise of decentralized data systems, blockchain technology, artificial intelligence, and quantum computing will introduce new paradigms for data storage, security, and analysis. Blockchain, for example, offers a transparent and tamper-proof way to manage digital transactions and records, reducing the risk of fraud and data manipulation.

Furthermore, the explosion of real-time data from IoT devices, 5G networks, and edge computing will accelerate the speed at which data flows through the Dataverse. Smart cities will leverage interconnected data to optimize energy consumption, reduce traffic congestion, and enhance public safety. AI-driven analytics will enable organizations to process vast amounts of unstructured data, extracting insights that were previously hidden.

Ultimately, the structure of the Dataverse is a reflection of the digital age—complex, ever-changing, and deeply intertwined with every aspect of human life. Understanding its layers and interactions will be crucial for harnessing the power of data, driving innovation, and shaping a future that is more data-driven, intelligent, and interconnected than ever before.

The Dynamics of Data Flow

One of the defining characteristics of the Dataverse is its dynamic nature. Data is not static; it is constantly flowing, changing, and interacting with other data in a complex, interconnected system. This continuous movement is driven by a variety of factors, including technological advancements, human behavior, economic activities, and natural phenomena. Unlike in the past, when data was primarily stored in physical formats such as books, ledgers, and archives, today's data ecosystem is characterized by instantaneous transmission and transformation across digital networks.

Technological advancements have played a crucial role in accelerating the flow of data. The rise of the internet, cloud computing, and wireless networks has made it possible to share information across the globe in real time. Social media platforms, for instance, have created an immense flow of data as billions of people share their thoughts, experiences, and opinions online every second. Every tweet, Facebook post, or Instagram story generates new data that feeds into the larger digital ecosystem. Similarly, the proliferation of smart devices and the Internet of Things (IoT) has led to an explosion of data as sensors and machines collect and transmit information about the physical world. From smart thermostats adjusting room temperatures based on occupancy patterns to wearable fitness trackers monitoring heart rates and activity levels, IoT devices contribute to a continuous stream of real-time data that shapes decision-making processes.

The flow of data is not limited to human-generated content; natural phenomena also contribute to the ever-expanding Dataverse. Satellites in space, weather monitoring stations, and geological sensors are constantly gathering data on climate patterns, seismic activities, and environmental changes. This data is crucial for predicting natural disasters, tracking climate change, and optimizing agricultural practices. For example, meteorological data collected from satellites and ground sensors is analyzed to provide early warnings about hurricanes, droughts, and extreme weather events, potentially saving lives and resources.

However, the movement of data is not a simple, one-way process. It is a complex, multi-directional system in which data is continuously created, shared, analyzed, and transformed across various platforms and industries. The interactions between different data sources create a network of information that evolves, leading to new insights and applications.

Consider a fitness tracker, which collects data on an individual's physical activity, heart rate, and sleep patterns. This data does not remain static within the device; it is often transmitted to cloud servers, where it can be accessed by healthcare providers, insurance companies, and researchers. A doctor might analyze the data to make personalized recommendations for improving the user's health. The same data could be aggregated with information from millions of other users to identify broader trends in physical activity and wellness, influencing public health policies and fitness industry strategies. Furthermore, the fitness tracker company might use machine learning algorithms to analyze user data and enhance product functionality, creating personalized fitness plans based on real-world usage patterns.

The interconnectivity of data extends beyond personal health devices. In the financial sector, stock market data flows through high-speed trading systems, where algorithms analyze price fluctuations in real-time to execute trades within microseconds. Banks and financial institutions rely on the continuous flow of data to assess risks, detect fraudulent transactions, and optimize investment portfolios. Similarly, in supply chain management, data from sensors embedded in shipping containers is transmitted to logistics companies, allowing them to track shipments, predict delays, and optimize delivery routes.

This intricate web of data flow highlights the importance of data interoperability, the ability of different systems to exchange and interpret data seamlessly. In many industries, the lack of standardization and integration challenges can hinder data flow, leading to inefficiencies and missed opportunities. For example, in the healthcare sector, patient records are often stored in different formats across hospitals, clinics, and insurance companies, making it difficult to share information efficiently. Efforts to standardize electronic health records (EHRs) aim to resolve this issue by ensuring that patient data can move freely between healthcare providers while maintaining security and privacy.

Understanding the dynamics of data flow is essential for managing and analyzing data effectively. It requires us to think about data not as a static resource but as a dynamic and interconnected system that evolves in response to technological, social, and environmental influences. By adopting this perspective, we can unlock new opportunities for insight and innovation. Businesses can leverage real-time data analytics to enhance decision-making, researchers can uncover hidden patterns that drive scientific discovery, and governments can use data-driven strategies to improve public services and urban planning.

The ability to harness the power of data flow also presents challenges. Privacy concerns, data security threats, and ethical considerations surrounding data usage must be carefully managed to ensure responsible data practices. The massive amounts of data being generated daily raise questions about who controls data, how it is used, and how individuals can protect their personal information in an increasingly digital world. Regulations such as the General Data Protection Regulation (GDPR) and the California Consumer Privacy Act (CCPA) have been introduced to address these concerns by giving individuals more control over their data and holding companies accountable for data handling practices.

As we move further into the digital age, the dynamics of data flow will continue to evolve. Emerging technologies such as edge computing, artificial intelligence, and 5G networks will enhance data transmission speed and processing capabilities, further accelerating the rate at which data flows through the Dataverse. Edge computing, for instance, enables data processing closer to its source—such as in a smart device or local server—rather than relying on distant cloud servers. This reduces latency and improves real-time data analytics, benefiting applications like autonomous vehicles, industrial automation, and real-time medical diagnostics.

In the future, the Dataverse will become even more integrated with human life, as data flows seamlessly between physical and digital realities. Smart cities will use interconnected data from traffic sensors, surveillance cameras, and energy grids to optimize urban living, reducing congestion, enhancing security, and improving sustainability. Advanced AI models will process massive datasets to provide personalized recommendations in entertainment, healthcare, and education. The rise of decentralized data systems powered by blockchain technology will offer new models of data ownership and security, allowing individuals to control how their personal information is shared and monetized.

Ultimately, the Dataverse is a living, breathing entity, constantly growing and adapting to new technologies, human interactions, and environmental changes. Recognizing and understanding the dynamics of data flow will be critical in shaping the future of industries, governments, and societies. By ensuring that data moves efficiently, securely, and ethically, we can unlock the full potential of the digital era, creating a world that is more connected, intelligent, and data-driven than ever before.

CHAPTER TWO

THE EVOLUTION OF DATA FROM ANALOG TO DIGITAL COSMOS

Long before the digital age, data existed in analog forms, etched into clay tablets, written on parchment, and later stored on magnetic tapes and vinyl records. These early methods of data storage were physical and tangible, relying on mechanical and electrical systems to capture and reproduce information. The analog era laid the foundation for the concept of data preservation, but it was limited by its susceptibility to degradation and its inability to scale efficiently. The invention of the telegraph and telephone marked the first steps toward transmitting data over distances, setting the stage for the revolutionary shift to digital. The advent of digital technology in the mid-20th century marked a seismic shift in how data was stored, processed, and transmitted. The introduction of binary code—a system of ones and zeros—allowed information to be represented in a universal language that machines could understand. This breakthrough enabled the development of computers, which could process data at unprecedented speeds and with remarkable accuracy. The digital revolution not only made data more durable and scalable but also democratized access to information, paving the way for the interconnected world we live in today. The creation of the internet in the late 20th century transformed data from a localized resource into a global phenomenon. For the first time, information could be shared instantly across vast distances, connecting people, businesses, and governments in ways that were previously unimaginable. The internet became the backbone of the digital cosmos, enabling the rise of email, e-commerce, and social media. This era also saw the birth of search engines, which organized the ever-growing expanse of digital data, making it accessible to anyone with an internet connection. As the digital universe expanded, so did the volume of data generate by individuals, organizations, and machines. The concept of "big data" emerged, referring to the massive datasets that could be analyzed to reveal patterns, trends, and insights. Advances in computing power and algorithms allowed businesses and researchers to harness this data, driving innovation in fields such as artificial intelligence, machine learning, and predictive analytics. The ability to process and interpret vast amounts of information transformed industries, from healthcare to finance, and reshaped decision-making processes on a global scale.

The Digital Cosmos: Data as the Fabric of Modern Life

Today, data is the lifeblood of the digital cosmos, permeating every aspect of our lives. From smart devices and wearable technology to cloud computing and the Internet of Things (IoT), data is continuously generated, collected, and analyzed in real time. This interconnected ecosystem has given rise to new possibilities, such as autonomous vehicles, personalized medicine, and smart cities.

However, it has also raised critical questions about privacy, security, and the ethical use of data. As we move forward, the evolution of data will continue to shape the future, driving innovation while challenging us to navigate the complexities of an increasingly digital world.

The interconnected ecosystem of data has fundamentally reshaped the way individuals, businesses, and governments operate, creating a world where digital intelligence drives decision-making, efficiency, and innovation. At the heart of this transformation is the constant flow of data generated by an ever-expanding network of devices and systems, each contributing to a larger digital framework that supports modern life.

Everyday technologies such as smartphones, smart homes, and autonomous vehicles are deeply embedded in this data-driven reality. Smartphones, for example, are not merely communication tools; they serve as gateways to vast amounts of information, enabling real-time navigation, online shopping, health tracking, and personalized entertainment. Smart homes further extend this connectivity by integrating IoT devices that automate household functions, from adjusting thermostats to optimizing energy consumption. Meanwhile, autonomous vehicles rely on complex algorithms and vast datasets to navigate roads safely, process traffic conditions, and interact with other smart infrastructure components in real time.

Businesses and organizations have come to rely on data as a strategic asset, leveraging analytics to optimize decision-making and improve operational efficiency. Companies use big data to gain insights into consumer behavior, tailoring products, and marketing campaigns to better align with customer preferences. Supply chain management has also been revolutionized, with predictive analytics enabling businesses to anticipate demand fluctuations, reduce waste, and improve logistics. In the financial sector, data-driven models enhance risk assessment, fraud detection, and algorithmic trading, ensuring that transactions are more secure and efficient.

Governments across the world have recognized the power of data in shaping policies, urban planning, and crisis response. Data-driven governance enables officials to assess population needs, allocate resources efficiently, and develop smart policies that improve public services. For instance, city planning now incorporates real-time traffic data to reduce congestion, while disaster response agencies use predictive analytics to anticipate and mitigate the impact of natural disasters. Public health initiatives also benefit from data integration, as disease tracking and epidemiological models help predict outbreaks and guide containment measures.

The healthcare industry in particular has undergone a profound transformation with the advent of data-driven solutions. Personalized medicine, powered by data analytics and artificial intelligence, allows treatments to be tailored to individual patients based on genetic profiles and medical histories. Predictive analytics enhances early disease detection, enabling healthcare providers to intervene before conditions worsen. Moreover, electronic health records streamline patient care by ensuring seamless data sharing among healthcare professionals, reducing errors, and improving treatment outcomes.

Cloud computing has played a pivotal role in enabling this vast digital ecosystem by providing the necessary infrastructure for real-time data storage, processing, and retrieval. Businesses and institutions no longer need to rely solely on on-premise servers, as cloud platforms offer scalable solutions that adapt to changing demands. This flexibility has facilitated the rapid growth of artificial intelligence, machine learning, and other data-intensive applications that require significant computational power.

The rise of IoT has further expanded the reach of data collection and utilization. Everyday objects, from refrigerators to industrial machinery, are now equipped with sensors that gather and transmit data, enhancing efficiency and automation. In industrial settings, predictive maintenance powered by IoT ensures that machines operate optimally, reducing downtime and operational costs. On a larger scale, entire city infrastructures have been transformed into interconnected networks, leading to the emergence of smart cities. In these urban environments, data-driven solutions enhance transportation systems, improve energy efficiency, and optimize public services. Smart traffic lights adjust based on real-time traffic conditions, waste management systems optimize collection routes using sensor data, and energy grids dynamically distribute power to reduce waste and lower costs.

Despite the numerous benefits of this interconnected data ecosystem, challenges remain, particularly concerning data privacy, security, and ethical considerations. As more personal and sensitive information is collected, the risk of cyber threats and data breaches grows. Striking a balance between innovation and data protection is crucial to maintaining public trust and ensuring that data-driven advancements benefit society without compromising individual privacy.

Ultimately, the modern world is being shaped by a complex, data-driven landscape where interconnectivity fuels progress across industries and sectors. As technologies continue to evolve and data becomes even more deeply integrated into daily life, the ability to harness, analyze, and secure this information will define the future of innovation, governance, and human interaction.

The Interconnected Ecosystem of Data

The interconnected ecosystem of data has fundamentally reshaped the way individuals, businesses, and governments operate, creating a world where digital intelligence drives decision-making, efficiency, and innovation. At the heart of this transformation is the constant flow of data generated by an ever-expanding network of devices and systems, each contributing to a larger digital framework that supports modern life.

Everyday technologies such as smartphones, smart homes, and autonomous vehicles are deeply embedded in this data-driven reality. Smartphones, for example, are not merely communication tools; they serve as gateways to vast amounts of information, enabling real-time navigation, online shopping, health tracking, and personalized entertainment. Smart homes further extend this connectivity by integrating IoT devices that automate household functions, from adjusting thermostats to optimizing energy consumption. Meanwhile, autonomous vehicles rely on complex algorithms and vast datasets to navigate roads safely, process traffic conditions, and interact with other smart infrastructure components in real time.

Businesses and organizations have come to rely on data as a strategic asset, leveraging analytics to optimize decision-making and improve operational efficiency. Companies use big data to gain insights into consumer behavior, tailoring products, and marketing campaigns to better align with customer preferences. Supply chain management has also been revolutionized, with predictive analytics enabling businesses to anticipate demand fluctuations, reduce waste, and improve logistics. In the financial sector, data-driven models enhance risk assessment, fraud detection, and algorithmic trading, ensuring that transactions are more secure and efficient.

Governments across the world have recognized the power of data in shaping policies, urban planning, and crisis response. Data-driven governance enables officials to assess population needs, allocate resources efficiently, and develop smart policies that improve public services. For instance, city planning now incorporates real-time traffic data to reduce congestion, while disaster response agencies use predictive analytics to anticipate and mitigate the impact of natural disasters. Public health initiatives also benefit from data integration, as disease tracking and epidemiological models help predict outbreaks and guide containment measures.

The healthcare industry in particular has undergone a profound transformation with the advent of data-driven solutions. Personalized medicine, powered by data analytics and artificial intelligence, allows treatments to be tailored to individual patients based on genetic profiles and medical histories. Predictive analytics enhances early disease detection, enabling healthcare providers to intervene before conditions worsen. Moreover, electronic health records streamline patient care by ensuring seamless data sharing among healthcare professionals, reducing errors, and improving treatment outcomes.

Cloud computing has played a pivotal role in enabling this vast digital ecosystem by providing the necessary infrastructure for real-time data storage, processing, and retrieval. Businesses and institutions no longer need to rely solely on on-premise servers, as cloud platforms offer scalable solutions that adapt to changing demands. This flexibility has facilitated the rapid growth of artificial intelligence, machine learning, and other data-intensive applications that require significant computational power.

The rise of IoT has further expanded the reach of data collection and utilization. Everyday objects, from refrigerators to industrial machinery, are now equipped with sensors that gather and transmit data, enhancing efficiency and automation. In industrial settings, predictive maintenance powered by IoT ensures that machines operate optimally, reducing downtime and operational costs. On a larger scale, entire city infrastructures have been transformed into interconnected networks, leading to the emergence of smart cities. In these urban environments, data-driven solutions enhance transportation systems, improve energy efficiency, and optimize public services. Smart traffic lights adjust based on real-time traffic conditions, waste management systems optimize collection routes using sensor data, and energy grids dynamically distribute power to reduce waste and lower costs.

Despite the numerous benefits of this interconnected data ecosystem, challenges remain, particularly concerning data privacy, security, and ethical considerations. As more personal and sensitive information is collected, the risk of cyber threats and data breaches grows. Striking a balance between innovation and data protection is crucial to maintaining public trust and ensuring that data-driven advancements benefit society without compromising individual privacy.

Ultimately, the modern world is being shaped by a complex, data-driven landscape where interconnectivity fuels progress across industries and sectors. As technologies continue to evolve and data becomes even more deeply integrated into daily life, the ability to harness, analyze, and secure this information will define the future of innovation, governance, and human interaction.

Transformative Possibilities Enabled by Data

The power of data has transcended mere convenience, driving transformative advancements across various industries and reshaping the way people interact with technology, services, and one another. Innovations that once seemed confined to science fiction are now realities, fueled by data-driven decision-making and predictive analytics. The integration of artificial intelligence, machine learning, and real-time data processing has led to groundbreaking progress in fields ranging from transportation and healthcare to finance, education, and entertainment.

Autonomous vehicles represent one of the most striking examples of how data is revolutionizing mobility. These self-driving systems rely on an intricate web of sensors, cameras, radar, and GPS technology to navigate roads with precision. By continuously processing real-time data, autonomous vehicles can detect obstacles, interpret traffic signals, and adjust to road conditions, all while improving safety and efficiency. Machine learning algorithms enhance their performance over time, allowing these vehicles to learn from past experiences and refine their decision-making processes. As the technology matures, self-driving cars have the potential to reduce traffic accidents, optimize fuel consumption, and transform urban transportation infrastructure.

In healthcare, data analytics is driving significant advancements in disease prevention, diagnosis, and treatment. Machine learning algorithms sift through vast amounts of patient data, identifying patterns that help predict disease outbreaks, customize treatment plans, and improve diagnostic accuracy. Personalized medicine, which tailor treatments to individual genetic profiles, has become increasingly feasible due to the ability to analyze large-scale genomic and clinical data. Predictive analytics also plays a critical role in early disease detection, enabling healthcare providers to intervene before conditions progress. Hospitals and research institutions leverage artificial intelligence to process medical imaging scans, detect abnormalities, and assist doctors in making more accurate diagnoses. Remote patient monitoring, powered by wearable devices, allows real-time health tracking and early intervention, ultimately improving patient outcomes and reducing the burden on healthcare facilities.

The financial sector has embraced data-driven strategies to enhance security, optimize investment decisions, and personalize customer experiences. Fraud detection systems analyze transaction patterns in real time, flagging suspicious activities before financial losses occur. Risk assessment models leverage data analytics to evaluate creditworthiness, ensuring that financial institutions make informed lending decisions. Personalized banking has also evolved, with AI-driven chatbots and recommendation engines offering tailored financial advice based on individual spending habits and preferences. Algorithmic trading relies on high-frequency data analysis, enabling investors to make split-second decisions that maximize returns while minimizing risks. The integration of blockchain technology further enhances security and transparency, ensuring that financial transactions are verifiable and immutable.

Education has seen a paradigm shift with the integration of data-driven technologies, creating personalized learning experiences that cater to individual student needs. Adaptive learning platforms use data analytics to track student progress, identify knowledge gaps, and adjust lesson plans accordingly. These systems provide real-time feedback, allowing educators to offer targeted support and interventions where necessary. Online learning platforms leverage AI-powered recommendations to suggest courses, supplementary materials, and study techniques tailored to a student's learning style. Additionally, data-driven insights help educational institutions optimize curricula, assess teaching effectiveness, and refine assessment methods. By harnessing the power of data, education is becoming more inclusive, accessible, and effective, ensuring that students receive the support they need to succeed.

The entertainment industry has also been revolutionized by data, with analytics playing a crucial role in content creation, distribution, and audience engagement. Streaming platforms analyze viewing habits, preferences, and user interactions to curate personalized recommendations that keep audiences engaged. Content creators use data-driven insights to determine which genres, themes, and formats resonate most with viewers, ensuring that productions align with audience expectations. The rise of artificial intelligence in content generation is evident in areas such as music composition, video editing, and scriptwriting, where algorithms assist in refining creative output. Virtual and augmented reality experiences are enhanced through data analytics, creating immersive entertainment that adapts to user behavior and preferences. Even in the gaming industry, real-time data processing enables dynamic in-game environments, responsive AI opponents, and personalized gameplay experiences.

The transformative possibilities enabled by data continue to evolve, shaping industries in ways that enhance efficiency, innovation, and personalization. As more sectors embrace data-driven technologies, the impact of these advancements will only grow, unlocking new opportunities for progress while also raising ethical and privacy considerations. The challenge lies in ensuring that data is harnessed responsibly, balancing innovation with security and trust. In an increasingly interconnected world, the ability to analyze, interpret, and apply data effectively will define the future of technological evolution and human progress.

Challenges and Ethical Considerations

The rapid expansion of data-driven technologies has brought about transformative benefits, yet it also presents significant ethical and security challenges that must be carefully managed. As businesses, governments, and individuals increasingly rely on data to drive decision-making, concerns about privacy, security, and the ethical use of artificial intelligence have taken center stage. The ability to collect, store, and analyze vast amounts of information has created an environment where personal data is constantly being tracked, often without the explicit consent or full awareness of the individuals involved. This has led to growing fears about surveillance, data exploitation, and the erosion of personal privacy in the digital age.

One of the most pressing concerns is the unauthorized collection and use of personal information. Many companies and online platforms track user behavior, preferences, and interactions to build detailed consumer profiles. While this data is often used to improve user experience, personalize recommendations, and optimize business operations, it can also be misused for targeted advertising, political manipulation, or even identity theft. Users frequently agree to complex and opaque privacy policies without fully understanding how their data will be used, shared, or monetized. In some cases, individuals have little to no control over their digital footprint, leading to a loss of autonomy over their personal information.

Data security is another critical issue, as cyberattacks and data breaches have become increasingly sophisticated and widespread. Organizations that store sensitive information, such as financial records, medical histories and personal identities, are prime targets for hackers. A single data breach can expose millions of users to fraud, identity theft, and financial loss, undermining trust in digital systems. High-profile cyberattacks on corporations, government agencies, and healthcare institutions have demonstrated the devastating consequences of inadequate security measures. The rise of ransomware attacks, where hackers encrypt valuable data and demand payment for their release, has further highlighted the urgent need for robust cybersecurity frameworks and proactive risk management strategies.

Beyond privacy and security, the ethical implications of artificial intelligence and machine learning algorithms have sparked intense debate. These technologies rely on vast datasets to make predictions and automate decision-making processes, but they are not immune to bias. If the underlying data is flawed or unrepresentative, AI systems can produce discriminatory or unfair outcomes. This is particularly concerning in areas such as hiring, lending, law enforcement, and healthcare, where biased algorithms can reinforce systemic inequalities. For example, AI-driven hiring platforms have been found to favor certain demographic groups over others, while predictive policing tools have disproportionately targeted marginalized communities. In the financial sector, biased credit scoring algorithms can limit access to loans for specific populations, further exacerbating economic disparities. Addressing these biases requires greater transparency in algorithmic design, rigorous testing for fairness, and ongoing oversight to ensure ethical decision-making.

Governments and regulatory bodies have introduced policies to mitigate these risks and protect individuals' rights in the digital landscape. The General Data Protection Regulation (GDPR), implemented in the European Union, is one of the most comprehensive data protection laws designed to give users greater control over their personal information. It mandates that organizations obtain clear consent before collecting data, provide transparency in data usage, and ensure the right to data portability and deletion. Other regions have adopted similar frameworks, such as the California Consumer Privacy Act (CCPA) in the United States, which grants consumers the right to know what data is being collected about them and the option to opt out of data sales. These regulations mark a significant step toward holding organizations accountable for ethical data practices, yet challenges remain in enforcing compliance across global digital platforms.

As technology continues to evolve, the challenge lies in striking a balance between innovation and ethical responsibility. Businesses must adopt privacy-by-design principles, embedding data protection measures into their products and services from the outset. Organizations should also prioritize ethical AI development by implementing bias detection methods, fostering diversity in data science teams, and establishing clear guidelines for responsible AI deployment. Additionally, there is a growing need for public awareness and digital literacy initiatives to educate users about their rights and the implications of data sharing.

Ultimately, the future of data-driven innovation depends on maintaining public trust and ensuring that technological advancements align with ethical standards. Governments, businesses, and civil society must work together to create policies and frameworks that protect individuals while enabling progress. The responsible use of data should prioritize transparency, fairness, and security, ensuring that data-driven technologies serve as tools for empowerment rather than instruments of exploitation. By addressing these challenges proactively, society can harness the full potential of data while safeguarding fundamental rights and values in the digital era.

The Future of Data and Digital Evolution

As society moves deeper into an era defined by digital transformation, the role of data will continue to expand, influencing industries, policy decisions, and the way individuals interact with technology. The sheer volume of data being generated every second is unprecedented, driven by advancements in artificial intelligence, the Internet of Things, and cloud computing. These developments have enabled seamless connectivity, real-time decision-making, and hyper-personalized experiences, but they have also raised new questions about security, ethics, and governance. The future of data lies not only in its growing influence but also in the way it is managed, secured, and leveraged for societal progress.

Emerging technologies are set to redefine the data landscape in profound ways. Quantum computing, for instance, holds the potential to revolutionize data processing capabilities by performing complex calculations at speeds that are impossible with traditional computers. This could significantly enhance encryption methods, optimize artificial intelligence models, and enable breakthroughs in fields such as materials science and pharmaceuticals. With the ability to analyze vast datasets almost instantaneously, quantum computing may unlock new scientific discoveries and accelerate advancements in machine learning. However, this power also comes with risks, particularly in the realm of cybersecurity, as quantum computers could theoretically break existing encryption standards, necessitating the development of quantum-resistant cryptographic techniques.

The advent of 6G networks will further enhance data connectivity, bringing ultra-fast speeds, lower latency, and improved reliability. Unlike previous generations of wireless networks, 6G will support real-time data exchange at an unprecedented scale, enabling innovations such as holographic communication, fully immersive virtual and augmented reality experiences, and seamless machine-to-machine interactions. This level of connectivity will empower industries by enabling autonomous systems, remote surgeries, and intelligent infrastructure capable of self-optimization. While 6G promises a future where digital and physical realities are more deeply intertwined, it also raises concerns about data privacy, surveillance, and the potential monopolization of digital infrastructure by a few powerful entities.

Blockchain technology is another key player in the future of data, offering decentralized and tamper-proof methods of recording and verifying information. By eliminating the need for intermediaries, blockchain enhances transparency, reduces fraud, and provides a more secure way to store and transfer data. Industries such as finance, healthcare, and supply chain management have already begun leveraging blockchain to improve security and trust in digital transactions. The integration of smart contracts—self-executing agreements written in code—further automates processes and minimizes the risk of manipulation. However, for blockchain to reach its full potential, challenges such as scalability, energy consumption, and regulatory acceptance must be addressed.

Artificial intelligence will continue to play a central role in shaping the digital future, making sense of massive datasets, and automating complex decision-making processes. AI-driven systems will become more intuitive, understanding human emotions, behaviors, and preferences with increasing accuracy. In healthcare, AI will refine diagnostic tools, predict disease outbreaks, and personalize treatment plans. In business, AI-powered analytics will drive more effective marketing strategies, enhance customer experiences, and streamline operations. Governments will use AI to improve public services, optimize urban planning, and enhance national security efforts. However, the ethical implications of AI must be carefully managed, ensuring that biases within algorithms do not perpetuate inequalities and that decisions made by machines remain transparent and accountable.

The future of data is not just about technological advancements but also about how society navigates the complex challenges that come with it. Cybersecurity will remain a top priority as cyber threats evolve in sophistication. Organizations will need to implement stronger data protection measures, invest in threat detection systems, and educate users on digital security best practices. Regulations will play a crucial role in ensuring that data is handled responsibly, with governments worldwide enacting policies to protect personal information and prevent misuse. Striking a balance between innovation and regulation will be critical to fostering a digital environment that is both secure and conducive to progress.

Transparency and ethical data practices will be essential in maintaining public trust. Companies and institutions must prioritize openness in how they collect, store, and use data, giving individuals greater control over their digital identities. Users should have the right to access, modify, and delete their data as they see fit, ensuring that their personal information is not exploited for profit or surveillance. Ethical AI frameworks will be necessary to guide the responsible development and deployment of intelligent systems, preventing discriminatory outcomes and ensuring that technology serves humanity rather than manipulates it.

As the digital landscape continues to evolve, the way society navigates this transformation will determine the extent to which data-driven innovations contribute to a more intelligent, efficient, and ethical world. By fostering responsible data practices, investing in robust cybersecurity measures, and prioritizing transparency, it is possible to harness the power of data to create a future that is not only technologically advanced but also equitable and sustainable. The digital revolution is a double-edged sword, offering both unprecedented opportunities and significant risks. The challenge lies in leveraging its potential while safeguarding the rights and freedoms of individuals. With a proactive and ethical approach, data can be a force for progress, enabling breakthroughs that benefit humanity for generations to come.

CHAPTER THREE

MAPPING THE TERRAINS DATA STRUCTURES AND ARCHITECTURE

Data structures serve as the building blocks of computer science, playing a fundamental role in organizing, storing, and managing data efficiently. Whether it is a simple array holding a list of elements or a complex graph representing intricate relationships, every data structure is designed to optimize operations such as searching, sorting, inserting, and deleting. Understanding these foundational structures is essential for designing efficient software systems, as the wrong choice of data structure can lead to performance bottlenecks and increased computational complexity.

At the simplest level, arrays provide a straightforward way to store elements in contiguous memory locations, allowing for constant-time access through indexing. However, they come with limitations, such as fixed size and expensive insertion and deletion operations that require shifting elements. Linked lists, on the other hand, offer dynamic memory allocation, allowing flexible resizing but at the cost of slower traversal due to the need for pointer navigation.

These two structures form the basis for more advanced structures like stacks and queues, which operate under the principles of Last-In-First-Out (LIFO) and First-In-First-Out (FIFO) respectively, making them useful for managing function calls, task scheduling, and buffer handling.

Moving to hierarchical structures, trees provide efficient ways to represent and manage hierarchical relationships. Binary trees, binary search trees (BSTs), and balanced trees such as AVL and Red-Black trees ensure optimal search, insertion, and deletion times by maintaining order within the nodes. Meanwhile, graphs take relational data representation to another level by enabling complex connectivity models and supporting applications such as social networking, navigation systems, and recommendation engines. Hash tables, with their ability to provide near-instantaneous lookups using key-value pairs, are heavily used in caching, database indexing, and distributed systems.

The efficient use of these data structures determines how effectively software handles data processing, making it crucial to select the right one for the right application.

I. Architectural Paradigms: Structuring the Flow of Data

The design of software and system architectures plays a fundamental role in determining how data flows within an application, how efficiently it is processed, and how securely it is stored. As the complexity of digital ecosystems grows, choosing the right architectural paradigm becomes essential for ensuring scalability, maintainability, and performance. The structure of an application dictates how its various components communicate, how data is managed across different layers, and how well the system can adapt to evolving demands. The choice of architecture depends on factors such as application requirements, expected user load, data processing needs, and the level of flexibility required for future modifications.

Traditional monolithic architectures have long been used in software development, where all components of an application—such as the user interface, business logic, and data storage—are tightly integrated into a single codebase. This design simplifies development and deployment, making it ideal for smaller applications with limited complexity. However, monolithic architectures can become difficult to scale and maintain as applications grow. Any modification to a single component may require redeploying the entire system, which can slow down development cycles and increase the risk of system failures.

To address the limitations of monolithic systems, microservices architecture has gained popularity, offering a modular approach where an application is composed of multiple independent services that communicate through APIs. Each microservice is responsible for a specific function, allowing teams to develop, deploy, and scale different components independently. This decoupled design enhances flexibility and resilience, as failures in one service do not necessarily impact the entire system. Microservices are particularly useful in large-scale applications with dynamic workloads, as they enable organizations to scale specific services as needed without affecting the rest of the system. However, implementing microservices introduces complexities in managing service communication, data consistency, and security, requiring careful orchestration through containerization technologies like Docker and Kubernetes.

Event-driven architecture represents another paradigm that structures the flow of data through asynchronous event-based communication. In this model, components respond to events rather than relying on direct service-to-service interactions. When an event occurs, such as a user placing an order or a sensor detecting a temperature change, an event broker captures and distributes the event to relevant services. This approach enhances scalability and responsiveness, making it well-suited for real-time applications, IoT systems, and financial transaction processing. By decoupling event producers and consumers, event-driven architectures improve system flexibility and resilience but introduce challenges in ensuring event ordering, consistency, and debugging.

Serverless computing takes a different approach by abstracting infrastructure management from developers, allowing them to focus solely on writing code while cloud providers handle the execution environment. In serverless architectures, applications are broken down into functions that are executed on demand in response to specific triggers. This model optimizes resource usage by scaling automatically based on workload, making it cost-efficient for applications with unpredictable traffic patterns. Serverless computing is ideal for microservices, API backends, and event-driven workflows, as it eliminates the need for provisioning and maintaining servers. However, latency introduced by cold starts, limitations in execution time, and vendor lock-in are factors that organizations must consider before adopting a fully serverless approach.

Data-centric architectures such as the Lambda and Kappa architectures have emerged to address challenges in big data processing. Lambda architecture combines batch and real-time processing to handle massive data workloads efficiently. It consists of three layers: the batch layer processes large volumes of historical data, the speed layer enables low-latency real-time analytics, and the serving layer provides query access to processed results. While Lambda architecture ensures accuracy and completeness in data analysis, it requires maintaining two separate processing pipelines, increasing development complexity. Kappa architecture, on the other hand, simplifies data processing by relying solely on real-time stream processing, eliminating the need for batch processing. This approach is advantageous for applications requiring continuous data ingestion and analysis, such as fraud detection, IoT analytics, and recommendation systems.

Choosing the right architectural paradigm is crucial for optimizing performance, scalability, and maintainability. Each architecture comes with trade-offs, and organizations must assess their specific needs to determine the most suitable approach. Factors such as data consistency requirements, system resilience, scalability expectations, and operational complexity play a significant role in architectural decisions. Hybrid architectures, which combine elements of multiple paradigms, are increasingly being adopted to leverage the strengths of different models while mitigating their limitations. As technology evolves, architectural paradigms will continue to adapt, shaping the future of data-driven applications and enabling new possibilities in digital innovation.

II. Monolithic Architecture

Monolithic architecture has been the foundation of software development for decades, providing a straightforward approach where all components of an application—user interface, business logic, and database access—are built, deployed, and maintained as a single, unified unit. This tightly integrated structure offers several advantages, particularly in the early stages of development, as it simplifies project setup, reduces inter-service communication overhead, and ensures consistency in business logic and data management. With everything contained in a single codebase, developers can easily manage dependencies, enforce business rules, and debug issues without needing to coordinate multiple services. This design also allows for efficient resource utilization since all functions of the application run within a single process, eliminating the complexity of distributed computing.

Despite these benefits, monolithic architectures present significant challenges as applications grow in complexity and scale. One of the primary drawbacks is the difficulty of scaling specific components independently. Since all modules are tightly coupled, increasing the capacity of a single feature requires scaling the entire application, which can be inefficient and resource intensive. This limitation often leads to performance bottlenecks, especially in large-scale applications that experience variable workloads across different functionalities. In contrast, modern architectures such as microservices allow for selective scaling, where only the most resource-intensive components are expanded based on demand.

Maintaining and updating a monolithic application becomes increasingly challenging over time. Because all features are interconnected within a single codebase, even minor modifications require the entire system to be rebuilt and redeployed. This makes continuous integration and continuous deployment (CI/CD) more cumbersome, slowing down the software development lifecycle. Developers working on different features may face dependency conflicts, and debugging can become time-consuming as issues in one module may have unintended consequences elsewhere in the system. As the codebase grows, onboarding new developers becomes more difficult, as they must understand the entire application rather than working on isolated components.

Another critical concern with monolithic architectures is the impact of a failure in one component on the entire system. Since all modules operate as part of a unified application, a single failure can cause the entire application to crash, leading to downtime and service disruptions. This lack of fault isolation makes monolithic systems less resilient compared to distributed architectures, where failures in one service do not necessarily impact others. Additionally, deploying new features or patches in a monolithic system often requires scheduling maintenance windows, as any update involves restarting the entire application. In contrast, modern architectures like microservices enable rolling updates and blue-green deployments, minimizing downtime and ensuring seamless user experiences.

Another limitation of monolithic systems is the difficulty of adopting new technologies or frameworks. Since all components are built using the same technology stack, transitioning to a new programming language, database, or development framework requires rewriting the entire application. This lack of flexibility can slow down innovation and make it harder for organizations to adapt to changing technological trends. In contrast, modular architectures such as microservices allow teams to experiment with different technologies for specific services without disrupting the overall application.

Security and compliance also present challenges in monolithic architectures. Because all modules share the same execution environment, vulnerabilities in one part of the system can expose the entire application to security risks. Implementing security measures such as role-based access control and encryption can be more complex, as they must be applied consistently across all layers of the monolith. Regulatory compliance becomes more difficult as well, especially in industries with strict data protection requirements, since ensuring granular access controls and auditing mechanisms within a monolithic structure can be cumbersome.

While monolithic architectures still have its place, particularly for smaller applications or projects with well-defined requirements, organizations aiming for scalability, flexibility, and rapid innovation are increasingly adopting microservices and other modular approaches. The transition from monolithic to microservices, however, requires careful planning, as breaking down a monolith into independent services involves challenges such as data consistency, service communication, and distributed transaction management. Some organizations opt for a hybrid approach, where critical components are extracted into microservices while maintaining a core monolithic structure for stability.

Ultimately, the choice of architecture depends on the specific needs of the application, team expertise, and long-term goals. Monolithic systems provide simplicity and ease of development in the short term but can lead to maintainability and scalability issues as applications grow. Organizations must weigh the trade-offs between the efficiency of monoliths and the flexibility of microservices to determine the most suitable architectural approach for their software development needs.

Microservices Architecture

Microservices architecture represents a fundamental shift from traditional monolithic software design, allowing applications to be developed as a collection of small, loosely coupled services that communicate through APIs. Each microservice is responsible for a specific business function, such as authentication, payment processing, or inventory management, and can be built, deployed, and scaled independently. This modular approach provides greater flexibility, making it easier for development teams to innovate and update applications without disrupting the entire system. Unlike monolithic architectures, where changes in one component often require redeploying the entire application, microservices enable incremental updates, reducing downtime and accelerating the software development lifecycle.

One of the key advantages of microservices is scalability. In a monolithic application, scaling involves replicating the entire system, even if only a single function, such as order processing or user authentication, is experiencing high traffic. This can be inefficient and costly. Microservices allow organizations to scale individual components based on demand. For example, an e-commerce platform experiencing a surge in checkout requests during a sale can allocate more resources to its payment service without affecting other parts of the application. This ability to scale services independently optimizes resource utilization and improves overall system performance.

Fault isolation is another major benefit of microservices. In a monolithic system, a failure in one part of the application can bring down the entire system, leading to significant downtime. With microservices, failures are contained within individual services, preventing widespread disruptions. If a recommendation engine fails on a streaming platform like Netflix, users can still browse and watch content while the faulty service is repaired. This resilience is particularly valuable for large-scale applications that require high availability and reliability.

The decentralized nature of microservices also enhances development efficiency. In a monolithic architecture, multiple teams often work on the same codebase, leading to dependency conflicts, longer development cycles, and difficulties in coordinating releases. Microservices allow teams to work independently on different services, choosing the most suitable programming languages, frameworks, and databases for their specific needs. This autonomy accelerates development, fosters innovation, and enables organizations to adopt new technologies without rewriting the entire application. Companies like Uber and Amazon have leveraged this approach to continuously evolve their platforms, introducing new features and optimizing performance without disrupting existing functionality.

Microservices also improve maintainability by simplifying codebases. Instead of managing a massive, interdependent application, developers focus on smaller, self-contained services that are easier to test, debug, and update. Automated testing and CI/CD pipelines further streamline development, ensuring that new features and bug fixes are deployed rapidly with minimal risk. Since each microservice is designed for a specific function, updates can be implemented without affecting unrelated components, reducing regression issues, and accelerating time-to-market for new features.

Despite its advantages, microservices introduce challenges that require careful management. Service communication complexity is a major consideration, as distributed systems rely on network-based interactions between services. API calls, message queues, and service discovery mechanisms must be optimized to ensure efficient data exchange. Latency and network failures can impact performance, making robust error-handling and fallback mechanisms essential. Tools like service meshes, load balancers, and distributed tracing frameworks help mitigate these challenges, providing better visibility and control over service interactions.

Data management is another complexity in microservices architecture. Unlike monolithic systems that typically use a single database, microservices often employ a decentralized data model where each service manages its own database. This improves flexibility and performance but introduces challenges in ensuring data consistency and integrity across services. Distributed transaction management, eventual consistency models, and event-driven messaging patterns are commonly used to handle these challenges. Organizations must carefully design their data architecture to balance performance, reliability, and consistency.

Security considerations in microservices are also more complex than in monolithic architectures. With multiple services communicating over a network, authentication, authorization, and encryption become critical concerns. Implementing secure API gateways, enforcing access controls, and monitoring service-to-service interactions help mitigate security risks. Additionally, managing multiple services requires effective orchestration, logging, and monitoring. Kubernetes, Docker, and containerization technologies play a crucial role in automating deployment, scaling, and maintenance of microservices, ensuring operational efficiency.

Organizations transitioning from monolithic to microservices architecture often adopt an incremental approach, gradually breaking down the monolith into independent services. This approach minimizes disruption and allows teams to address integration challenges as they arise. While microservices offer significant benefits in terms of scalability, agility, and resilience, they require a well-thought-out strategy for service communication, data management, security, and operational monitoring. Companies that successfully implement microservices, such as Netflix, Uber, and Amazon, have demonstrated how this architecture can transform digital platforms, enabling them to handle millions of user requests efficiently while continuously evolving to meet customer demands.

Data-Centric Architectures

Data-centric architectures prioritize the efficient handling, storage, and processing of data, making it the core around which applications and business logic revolve. Unlike traditional architectures that focus on application functionality first, data-centric systems are designed to manage vast amounts of structured and unstructured data while ensuring consistency, accessibility, and integrity. This architectural approach is particularly valuable in environments that rely on big data analytics, artificial intelligence, and machine learning, where deriving insights from massive datasets is a fundamental requirement.

One of the defining characteristics of data-centric architectures is their reliance on powerful database management systems and distributed storage solutions. These systems enable organizations to store, retrieve, and process data efficiently, even as the volume and complexity of data grow. Relational databases like PostgreSQL and MySQL are commonly used for structured data, ensuring ACID (Atomicity, Consistency, Isolation, Durability) compliance and maintaining strong data integrity. However, as data requirements have evolved, NoSQL databases such as MongoDB, Cassandra, and DynamoDB have become increasingly popular for handling semi-structured and unstructured data. These databases offer flexible schema designs, horizontal scalability, and high availability, making them well-suited for real-time applications, content management systems, and large-scale analytics platforms.

Scalability is a crucial aspect of data-centric architectures, as modern applications must handle exponential data growth. Distributed storage technologies such as Apache Hadoop, Apache HBase, and Google Bigtable allow data to be partitioned across multiple nodes, enabling parallel processing and fault tolerance. Cloud-based storage solutions like Amazon S3, Google Cloud Storage, and Azure Blob Storage provide virtually unlimited storage capacity, making it easier for organizations to manage and process large datasets without investing in costly on-premises infrastructure. By leveraging distributed storage, applications can handle petabytes of data while ensuring redundancy and failover mechanisms to prevent data loss.

Data processing in data-centric architectures requires robust pipelines that can ingest, transform, and analyze data efficiently. Technologies such as Apache Spark and Apache Flink enable real-time and batch data processing, allowing organizations to extract valuable insights from data streams. These frameworks support distributed computing, enabling parallel execution of data processing tasks across clusters of machines. Streaming platforms like Apache Kafka and AWS Kinesis facilitate real-time data ingestion, ensuring that applications can process continuous streams of data generated by sensors, user interactions, financial transactions, and other sources. By integrating streaming and batch processing, organizations can build dynamic analytics pipelines that support real-time decision-making and predictive modeling.

Artificial intelligence and machine learning applications greatly benefit from data-centric architectures, as they require vast amounts of high-quality data to train and optimize models. Data lakes, such as those built on Amazon Lake Formation or Apache Iceberg, provide centralized repositories for raw and processed data, enabling data scientists to access and experiment with diverse datasets. Feature stores help standardize data for machine learning models, ensuring consistency and reusability across different AI applications. Additionally, model deployment platforms like TensorFlow Serving and MLflow facilitate seamless integration of trained models into production systems, allowing organizations to leverage AI-driven insights in real-world scenarios.

Ensuring data consistency and integrity is a critical challenge in data-centric architectures. In distributed systems, maintaining strong consistency across multiple data nodes can introduce latency, leading many organizations to adopt eventual consistency models where updates propagate over time. Techniques such as conflict-free replicated data types (CRDTs) and distributed consensus algorithms like Paxos and Raft help manage consistency across distributed environments. Implementing data governance frameworks is also essential, as organizations must enforce policies for data access, security, and compliance with regulations like GDPR and CCPA. Data lineage tracking, audit logging, and encryption mechanisms enhance security and accountability, ensuring that sensitive information is protected.

The rise of cloud computing has further transformed data-centric architectures, enabling organizations to build scalable, cost-effective data ecosystems. Cloud-native databases such as Amazon Aurora, Google Spanner, and Microsoft Cosmos DB offer managed database solutions with automatic scaling, backup, and high availability. Serverless data processing services like AWS Lambda and Google Cloud Functions provide event-driven compute capabilities, allowing organizations to process data dynamically without managing infrastructure. Hybrid and multi-cloud strategies enable businesses to distribute their data workloads across different cloud providers, optimizing performance, cost, and redundancy.

Data-centric architectures are fundamental to industries that rely on data-driven decision-making. In finance, real-time risk analysis and fraud detection depend on fast, accurate data processing. In healthcare, genomic research and personalized medicine require vast datasets to be analyzed efficiently. E-commerce platforms use recommendation engines powered by data-centric architectures to enhance user experiences. Autonomous vehicles and smart cities leverage data streams from sensors and IoT devices to optimize traffic flow, improve safety, and reduce energy consumption.

While data-centric architectures provide powerful capabilities, they require careful planning and implementation to maximize efficiency. Organizations must design their data pipelines to handle large-scale ingestion, transformation, and analysis while ensuring performance, security, and compliance. The integration of distributed storage, real-time processing, AI-driven analytics, and cloud-native solutions continues to push the boundaries of what data-centric architectures can achieve. As businesses increasingly rely on data to drive innovation and competitive advantage, adopting a well-structured data-centric approach will be key to unlocking new possibilities in the digital age.

Serverless Architecture

Serverless architecture represents a paradigm shift in system design by eliminating the need for developers to manage underlying infrastructure, enabling them to focus purely on application logic. Unlike traditional server-based deployments, where organizations must provision, maintain, and scale servers, serverless computing allows applications to run in fully managed environments where cloud providers handle execution, scaling, and availability. This model ensures that computing resources are allocated dynamically, and organizations are only billed for the actual execution time of their code rather than maintaining persistent infrastructure that may remain underutilized.

At the core of serverless architecture are function-as-a-service (FaaS) platforms such as AWS Lambda, Google Cloud Functions, and Azure Functions. These services enable developers to break applications into discreet, event-driven functions that execute in stateless environments. Functions are triggered by specific events, such as HTTP requests, database updates, file uploads, or message queue events, and automatically scale based on demand. This event-driven nature makes serverless particularly well-suited for applications with highly variable workloads, such as web applications handling sporadic traffic spikes, IoT data processing, and real-time analytics.

One of the primary advantages of serverless computing is its cost efficiency. Traditional server-based models require organizations to provision servers with enough capacity to handle peak traffic, leading to inefficiencies when demand fluctuates. With serverless, organizations are only charged for the actual compute time used by their functions, eliminating costs associated with idle resources. This pay-as-you-go model is especially beneficial for startups, small businesses, and applications with unpredictable traffic patterns, as it significantly reduces infrastructure expenses.

Scalability is another defining feature of serverless architecture. Cloud providers automatically scale functions up or down in response to incoming requests, ensuring applications remain highly responsive even during sudden traffic surges. Unlike monolithic applications that require manual scaling strategies, serverless architectures allow each function to scale independently, optimizing performance and resource utilization. This built-in scalability is particularly advantageous for applications such as chatbots, which must handle fluctuating user interactions, and real-time notifications, where low-latency responses are critical.

By abstracting away infrastructure management, serverless architectures also reduce operational complexity. Developers no longer need to worry about provisioning servers, configuring load balancers, or performing routine maintenance tasks such as patching and security updates. This streamlining accelerates development cycles, enabling faster innovation and shorter time-to-market for new features. Continuous deployment and integration (CI/CD) pipelines can be seamlessly integrated with serverless functions, allowing organizations to deploy updates with minimal downtime and risk.

Serverless architectures are highly compatible with microservices, as both emphasize modularity and independent scalability. Organizations transitioning from monolithic applications to microservices can leverage serverless to deploy specific services as individual functions, reducing overhead and increasing flexibility. Additionally, serverless functions integrate well with API gateways, enabling developers to expose functions as RESTful or GraphQL endpoints that serve frontend applications efficiently. This approach is particularly useful for single-page applications (SPAs) and mobile backends, where lightweight and scalable APIs are essential.

Despite its advantages, serverless computing introduces unique challenges that must be carefully managed. Cold start latency is a common concern, as serverless functions that have not been recently invoked may experience initial delays when spinning up new execution environments. While cloud providers optimize cold start times through techniques such as provisioned concurrency, latency-sensitive applications must consider alternative strategies such as keeping functions warm through periodic invocations.

Another challenge is state management. Serverless functions operate in stateless environments, meaning they do not retain information between executions. While this design improves scalability, it requires external solutions for managing persistent data. Cloud-based storage services such as Amazon S3, DynamoDB, Firebase, and Redis are commonly used to store session data, application states, and user preferences. Additionally, event-driven architectures often leverage message queues and event streaming platforms like AWS SQS, Google Pub/Sub, and Apache Kafka to coordinate workflows between serverless functions.

Security considerations in serverless computing differ from traditional architectures. Since functions execute in ephemeral environments, organizations must implement strong authentication and authorization mechanisms to prevent unauthorized access. Identity and Access Management (IAM) policies, role-based access controls (RBAC), and API gateways help enforce security best practices. Additionally, serverless applications are susceptible to denial-of-service (DoS) attacks if not properly configured, as automatic scaling can lead to excessive resource consumption under malicious traffic loads. Implementing rate limiting, request validation, and anomaly detection can mitigate such risks.

Observability and debugging in serverless environments also present challenges, as traditional monitoring tools designed for persistent servers may not provide sufficient visibility into function execution. Cloud providers offer built-in logging and monitoring solutions, such as AWS CloudWatch, Google Cloud Logging, and Azure Monitor, to help track function performance, execution times, and error rates. Distributed tracing tools like AWS X-Ray and OpenTelemetry further assist in diagnosing performance bottlenecks and identifying dependencies within serverless applications.

Serverless computing is transforming how organizations build and deploy applications across various industries. In e-commerce, serverless enables dynamic scaling of product recommendation engines and checkout processes, ensuring seamless user experiences even during peak shopping seasons. In media and entertainment, serverless powers real-time video processing and personalized content delivery. In finance, serverless facilitates fraud detection and automated transaction processing by analyzing vast datasets in real time. The healthcare industry benefits from serverless through scalable telemedicine platforms, AI-driven diagnostics, and secure patient data management.

As serverless technologies continue to evolve, hybrid and multi-cloud strategies are becoming increasingly popular. Organizations are adopting a mix of serverless and traditional architectures to balance cost, performance, and control. Edge computing is also emerging as a complementary trend, where serverless functions execute closer to end-users to minimize latency and enhance performance for applications such as IoT analytics and augmented reality.

Serverless architecture represents a major evolution in cloud computing, enabling organizations to build highly scalable, cost-efficient, and resilient applications. By abstracting away infrastructure concerns, optimizing resource allocation, and integrating seamlessly with modern development practices, serverless empowers developers to focus on innovation rather than infrastructure management. While challenges such as cold starts, state management, and security must be addressed, the benefits of serverless computing make it an increasingly attractive option for organizations looking to build agile, event-driven applications in the cloud-driven digital era.

Optimizing Performance with Efficient Data Structures

Choosing the right data structure directly impacts the efficiency and speed of an application. For example, when performing frequent searches, hash tables offer constant-time lookups, making them indispensable for implementing caches, dictionaries, and database indexing. In contrast, binary search trees (BSTs) and B-trees provide structured ways to store and retrieve data efficiently, making them essential for databases and file systems.

Graph-based structures play a significant role in modeling networks, whether for internet routing, social networks, or logistics. The ability to traverse these structures efficiently using algorithms like Dijkstra's shortest path or Depth-First Search (DFS) ensures optimal performance in solving complex real-world problems.

Memory efficiency is another key factor in performance optimization. Sparse matrices help conserve memory when dealing with predominantly zero-valued datasets, while compressed tries and prefix trees enhance storage efficiency for text-based applications like autocomplete and spell-checking systems. Balancing time complexity and space complexity is critical, as some algorithms optimize speed at the expense of higher memory usage, whereas others prioritize conserving memory at the cost of slower execution.

Scalability and Data Management in Modern Architectures

Scalability is a fundamental requirement for modern applications, especially as data volumes continue to grow exponentially. Traditional relational databases such as MySQL and PostgreSQL follow strict ACID (atomicity, consistency, isolation, durability) principles, ensuring reliability in transactional systems. However, these databases can struggle with horizontal scaling, leading to the rise of NoSQL databases like MongoDB, Cassandra, and DynamoDB, which offer flexible schemas and improved scalability.

Cloud computing has further transformed data management, enabling applications to scale dynamically based on demand. Technologies like Amazon S3, Google Big Query, and Microsoft Azure Cosmos DB provide distributed storage solutions that handle petabytes of data while ensuring high availability and redundancy. Distributed storage systems like Hadoop and Apache Cassandra ensures fault tolerance by replicating data across multiple nodes, allowing seamless recovery in case of hardware failures.

With the rise of streaming data, real-time processing frameworks such as Apache Kafka and Apache Flink allow businesses to process and analyze continuous data streams, making them valuable for applications like fraud detection, stock market analysis, and sensor data monitoring. The integration of edge computing further enhances scalability by processing data closer to its source, reducing latency and minimizing bandwidth usage.

Future Perspectives: Emerging Trends in Data Structures and Architectures

As technology evolves, new trends in data structures and architectures continue to emerge, shaping the future of computing. One of the most groundbreaking areas is AI-driven data structures, where machine learning algorithms optimize data organization dynamically, improving search speeds and predictive analytics. AI-powered indexing mechanisms and intelligent caching strategies are revolutionizing how applications manage large-scale data.

Another disruptive innovation is quantum computing, which introduces entirely new paradigms for data storage and computation. Traditional data structures may become obsolete as quantum states enable parallel processing on an unprecedented scale, potentially solving complex problems in seconds that would take classical computers years.

Blockchain architecture is redefining data security and decentralization by enabling tamper-proof, distributed ledgers. Industries such as finance, supply chain management, and digital identity verification are leveraging blockchain to enhance transparency and reduce fraud.

Additionally, serverless computing is gaining traction, allowing developers to execute code without provisioning or managing servers. This model optimizes cost and scalability, making it ideal for microservices and event-driven applications.

The continuous evolution of data structures and architectures underscores the importance of staying ahead of technological advancements. Whether in AI, quantum computing, or decentralized systems, the ability to adapt and leverage new approaches will determine success in the ever-changing landscape of data-driven innovation.

CHAPTER FOUR

CHARTING THE CURRENTS DATA FLOW AND INTERCONNECTIVITY

In today's digital landscape, data serves as the lifeblood of our interconnected world, seamlessly flowing through networks, systems, and devices to power nearly every aspect of modern life. Much like an invisible current, data moves continuously, shaping our experiences, driving technological advancements, and influencing decisions at both individual and global levels. From personalized recommendations on streaming platforms to real-time financial transactions and AI-driven insights, the way data travels and interacts within digital ecosystems determines the efficiency, security, and intelligence of our digital experiences. Understanding the pathways, patterns, and underlying mechanisms of data flow, as well as the intricate web of interconnectivity that facilitates it, is essential for navigating the complexities of today's information-driven environment. By grasping how data is collected, processed, and exchanged across platforms, we gain the ability to harness its power effectively—whether for innovation, strategic decision-making, or ensuring ethical and responsible data usage in an increasingly digital world.

Sources and Generation: The Origins of Data

Data generation is a fundamental aspect of the digital world, with vast amounts of information created every second from diverse sources. Human interactions with digital devices, such as smartphones, computers, and wearable technology, contribute significantly to data creation. Every online search, social media post, e-commerce transaction, and digital communication generates data points that fuel various applications, from personalized marketing to artificial intelligence.

Beyond human-generated data, the proliferation of the Internet of Things (IoT) has introduced another massive stream of machine-generated data. IoT devices, including smart home appliances, industrial sensors, and connected vehicles, continuously collect and transmit data for automation, monitoring, and decision-making. For example, smart thermostats learn user preferences to optimize energy efficiency, while industrial IoT sensors track equipment performance to predict maintenance needs. Scientific research and experiments also produce enormous volumes of data. Fields such as genomics, climate science, and particle physics rely on high-throughput data generation. For instance, the Large Hadron Collider (LHC) at CERN produces petabytes of data annually from particle collision experiments, requiring sophisticated data processing and storage solutions. In healthcare, medical imaging, genomic sequencing, and patient records contribute to expanding data repositories, aiding in diagnostics and personalized medicine.

The rapid explosion of data from these sources highlights the need for efficient data management, transmission, and processing strategies. Social media platforms process billions of user interactions daily, while enterprises collect structured and unstructured data from sales, customer interactions, and operational workflows. As the digital ecosystem continues to expand, understanding how data moves through networks and systems becomes crucial for harnessing its full potential.

Data Transmission and Routing: The Journey of Information

Once data is generated, it must be transmitted across networks to reach its intended destination. The process of data transmission involves multiple layers of communication protocols, infrastructure components, and routing mechanisms that ensure seamless delivery. At the core of data transmission is the Transmission Control Protocol/Internet Protocol (TCP/IP), which defines how data packets travel across the internet. When a user sends an email, loads a webpage, or streams a video, the data is broken into packets and transmitted through a network of routers and switches. These packets traverse various network paths before being reassembled at their destination.

The internet relies on a complex infrastructure of fiber optic cables, wireless networks, and satellite connections to facilitate data movement. Fiber optic technology enables high-speed data transmission over long distances, while wireless networks such as Wi-Fi and 5G enhance mobility and connectivity. Cloud computing has further optimized data transmission by reducing latency and providing distributed access to resources.

Routing plays a critical role in determining the optimal path for data packets. Dynamic routing protocols such as Border Gateway Protocol (BGP) and Open Shortest Path First (OSPF) enable routers to make real-time decisions based on network conditions. Content delivery networks (CDNs) further enhance data transmission by catching frequently accessed content in geographically distributed data centers, reducing load times for users worldwide.

As data transmission becomes more sophisticated, security concerns such as encryption, cybersecurity threats, and network resilience must be addressed. Secure communication protocols such as HTTPS, VPNs, and end-to-end encryption protect sensitive information from unauthorized access. Additionally, technologies like edge computing reduce latency by processing data closer to the source, improving real-time applications such as self-driving cars and remote medical diagnostics.

Data Storage and Processing: From Raw Data to Insights

After transmission, data must be efficiently stored and processed to extract meaningful insights. Over the years, data storage technologies have evolved from traditional relational databases to highly scalable cloud-based and distributed storage solutions.

Traditional database systems like MySQL, PostgreSQL, and Oracle have long been the foundation of structured data storage, ensuring consistency, integrity, and reliability. However, with the rise of unstructured data from images, videos, and social media feeds, alternative storage solutions such as NoSQL databases (MongoDB, Cassandra, DynamoDB) have gained popularity. These systems offer flexibility in schema design, horizontal scalability, and high availability.

Cloud computing has revolutionized data storage by offering on-demand, scalable storage solutions through services like Amazon S3, Google Cloud Storage, and Microsoft Azure Blob Storage. Cloud-based storage eliminates the need for organizations to maintain physical infrastructure while ensuring data redundancy and security through distributed architectures.

Once stored, data must be processed to generate actionable insights. Batch processing and real-time analytics represent two primary methods of data processing. Batch processing, used in applications such as financial reporting and historical data analysis, involves processing large datasets at scheduled intervals. Frameworks like Apache Hadoop and Apache Spark enable efficient batch data processing across distributed systems.

Conversely, real-time analytics is essential for applications that require immediate data processing, such as fraud detection, recommendation systems, and live monitoring. Stream processing frameworks like Apache Flink, Apache Kafka, and Google Dataflow facilitate real-time data ingestion and analysis, allowing businesses to make instant data-driven decisions.

Machine learning and artificial intelligence further enhance data processing by identifying patterns, predicting outcomes, and automating decision-making. AI-powered analytics platforms process vast datasets to uncover trends, personalize user experiences, and optimize business strategies. For instance, AI-driven chatbots use natural language processing (NLP) to analyze customer interactions and provide automated responses.

Data storage and processing strategies continue to evolve with advancements in edge computing, serverless architectures, and quantum computing. These innovations enable faster, more efficient data handling while addressing the challenges of scalability, security, and computational complexity.

Data Consumption and Utilization: Driving Decisions and Innovation

The final stage of data flow involves how information is consumed, analyzed, and utilized to drive decision-making and innovation. Individuals, organizations, and applications rely on data visualization, reporting, and automation to transform raw data into meaningful insights.

Data visualization plays a crucial role in making complex data more accessible. Tools such as Tableau, Power BI, and Google Data Studio enable businesses to create interactive dashboards that highlight key metrics, trends, and patterns. Well-designed visualizations help stakeholders interpret data efficiently, supporting informed decision-making across industries.

Organizations leverage data for business intelligence (BI), predictive analytics, and operational optimization. BI platforms aggregate data from multiple sources to provide real-time performance monitoring, while predictive analytics uses historical data to forecast future trends. For example, e-commerce platforms analyze customer behavior to recommend products, while logistics companies optimize supply chain routes using predictive models.

Automated decision-making powered by AI and machine learning is reshaping industries such as finance, healthcare, and cybersecurity. Fraud detection systems analyze transaction patterns to flag suspicious activities, while AI-powered diagnostics assist doctors in identifying diseases from medical images. In cybersecurity, machine learning models detect anomalies in network traffic to prevent data breaches and cyberattacks.

The rise of data-driven products and services has transformed user experiences. From personalized content recommendations on Netflix and Spotify to AI-driven voice assistants like Siri and Alexa, data fuels innovation in entertainment, communication, and automation. Smart cities leverage data to optimize traffic flow, reduce energy consumption, and enhance public safety, creating more efficient urban environments.

As data continues to shape the future, the challenge lies in striking a balance between technological advancement and ethical responsibility. By fostering responsible data practices, businesses and governments can harness the power of data to build a more intelligent, efficient, and inclusive digital ecosystem.

2. The Web of Interconnectivity:

Network Topologies and Architectures: The Foundation of Digital Communication

The structure of networks plays a crucial role in determining how efficiently data flows between devices, systems, and users. Network topology refers to the physical or logical arrangement of devices in a network, influencing aspects such as reliability, scalability, and data transmission speed. Different topologies are used in various contexts based on their advantages and limitations.

In a star topology, all devices connect to a central hub or switch, which manages communication between nodes. This structure is common in local area networks (LANs) due to its simplicity and ease of troubleshooting. However, the failure of the central hub can disrupt the entire network. Mesh topology, on the other hand, ensures redundancy by connecting every device to multiple other devices. This design enhances reliability and fault tolerance, making it ideal for mission-critical applications like military communications and financial systems. Bus topology, in which all devices share a single communication channel, was historically used in early computer networks but has been largely replaced due to scalability issues.

At a larger scale, the architecture of the internet defines how global data transmission occurs. Internet Service Providers (ISPs) act as intermediaries, connecting end-users to the broader internet. ISPs rely on a hierarchy, with Tier 1 ISPs forming the backbone of the internet by maintaining global fiber-optic infrastructure. Tier 2 and Tier 3 ISPs connect businesses and consumers to this backbone, routing data through a network of interconnected servers.

Data centers play a crucial role in internet infrastructure, hosting cloud services, enterprise applications, and online content. These large-scale facilities house thousands of servers, ensuring high availability and redundancy for data storage and processing. To improve content delivery and reduce latency, Content Delivery Networks (CDNs) distribute copies of web content across multiple data centers worldwide. Companies like Akamai, Cloudflare, and

AWS CloudFront use CDNs to ensure that users can access data from the nearest geographical location, speeding up load times and optimizing performance.

The architecture of networks and the internet is designed to prioritize speed, reliability, and redundancy, ensuring that data flows seamlessly even under high traffic conditions. As digital connectivity expands, advancements in network topologies and architectures will continue to shape the future of global communication.

The Internet of Things (IoT) and Edge Computing: A Revolution in Data Processing

The emergence of the Internet of Things (IoT) has transformed how data is generated, processed, and utilized. IoT refers to a network of interconnected devices—ranging from smart home appliances to industrial sensors—that collect and exchange data to improve efficiency, automation, and decision-making.

IoT devices continuously transmit vast amounts of data, enabling applications such as smart cities, industrial automation, healthcare monitoring, and connected vehicles. Smart home ecosystems, powered by devices like Google Nest and Amazon Alexa, integrate IoT sensors to control lighting, security, and temperature based on user preferences. In industrial settings, IoT-enabled sensors track equipment performance, predicting failures and optimizing maintenance schedules to reduce downtime.

As IoT adoption grows, the need for real-time data processing has led to the rise of edge computing. Traditional cloud computing models rely on centralized data centers, which can introduce latency when processing time-sensitive information. Edge computing shifts data processing closer to the source—on local devices or edge servers—reducing response times and bandwidth usage.

For example, autonomous vehicles require real-time decision-making capabilities, such as identifying pedestrians and traffic signals. By leveraging edge computing, self-driving cars can process sensor data locally instead of sending it to remote servers, enabling rapid responses. Similarly, smart factories use edge computing to analyze production line data in real time, detecting defects and optimizing manufacturing processes.

The combination of IoT and edge computing is paving the way for faster, more responsive, and intelligent systems across industries. However, challenges such as security vulnerabilities, device interoperability, and data privacy concerns must be addressed to ensure the reliability and trustworthiness of these interconnected systems.

Cloud Computing and Data Sharing: The Backbone of the Digital Economy

Cloud computing has redefined how organizations store, process, and share data. Instead of relying on physical servers, businesses and individuals can access computing resources on demand through cloud service providers like Amazon Web Services (AWS), Microsoft Azure, and Google Cloud Platform (GCP).

One of the biggest advantages of cloud computing is scalability. Organizations can dynamically adjust their computing resources based on demand, ensuring cost efficiency and operational flexibility. This capability is particularly valuable for businesses with fluctuating workloads, such as e-commerce platforms that experience seasonal spikes in traffic.

Cloud computing enables seamless data sharing and collaboration, allowing multiple users to access and edit documents in real time. Services like Google Drive, Dropbox, and Microsoft OneDrive have revolutionized workplace productivity, eliminating the need for physical storage devices and enabling remote collaboration. In enterprise environments, cloud-based customer relationship management (CRM) platforms, such as Salesforce, centralize customer data to enhance business intelligence and decision-making.

Despite its benefits, cloud computing also presents challenges, particularly in data security and privacy. Storing sensitive information in the cloud increases the risk of cyberattacks and unauthorized access. To mitigate these risks, organizations implement encryption, multi-factor authentication (MFA), and compliance measures such as the General Data Protection Regulation (GDPR) to protect user data.

As cloud adoption continues to expand, innovations such as hybrid cloud and multi-cloud strategies are emerging. Hybrid cloud solutions combine on-premises infrastructure with cloud services, offering businesses greater flexibility and control over their data. Multi-cloud architectures, where companies use multiple cloud providers, reduce vendor dependency, and enhance resilience.

The future of cloud computing will be shaped by advancements in serverless computing, AI-driven cloud automation, and quantum computing, further enhancing the efficiency and intelligence of cloud-based data management.

APIs and Data Integration: The Glue That Connects Digital Systems

In an increasingly interconnected digital landscape, Application Programming Interfaces (APIs) play a crucial role in enabling seamless communication between different applications, services, and platforms. APIs act as intermediaries that allow software components to exchange data and functionality, facilitating integration between systems.

APIs power a wide range of modern digital services, from social media integrations (e.g., embedding Twitter feeds on websites) to payment gateways (e.g., PayPal and Stripe enabling secure online transactions). In e-commerce, APIs allow businesses to connect inventory management systems with online marketplaces, ensuring real-time stock updates.

One of the most significant applications of APIs is in data integration, where organizations consolidate data from multiple sources to create a unified and cohesive ecosystem. RESTful APIs and GraphQL enable applications to retrieve and manipulate data efficiently, improving interoperability across platforms.

For example, healthcare providers use APIs to integrate electronic health records (EHRs) with diagnostic tools, enabling doctors to access patient data from different hospitals in a standardized format. In finance, Open Banking APIs allow third-party apps to connect with banking systems, providing users with a unified view of their financial accounts and personalized financial insights.

However, API security is a growing concern, as improperly secured APIs can expose sensitive data to cyber threats. Organizations implement authentication mechanisms such as OAuth, API keys, and rate limiting to prevent unauthorized access and data breaches.

As digital transformation accelerates, API-first strategies are becoming essential for businesses seeking to enhance agility and scalability. The rise of AI-driven APIs, blockchain-based integrations, and API marketplaces will further expand the possibilities for seamless and secure data exchange.

Data Security and Privacy: Safeguarding Information in an Interconnected World

As the digital ecosystem grows more interconnected, data security and privacy concerns have become critical challenges for individuals, businesses, and governments. The vast amount of personal, financial, and corporate data being generated and shared daily presents lucrative opportunities for cybercriminals and increases the risk of unauthorized access, data breaches, and cyberattacks.

Common Security Threats and Cyber Risks

One of the most pervasive threats in today's digital landscape is data breaches, where malicious actors gain unauthorized access to sensitive information. High-profile incidents, such as the Equifax breach and Facebook's data exposure, have demonstrated the devastating impact of poor security measures, leading to financial losses, reputational damage, and regulatory fines. Cyberattacks, including ransomware, phishing, and Distributed Denial-of-Service (DDoS) attacks, further threaten the integrity of digital systems. These attacks can cripple businesses, disrupt critical infrastructure, and compromise national security.

To combat these risks, organizations must adopt robust cybersecurity strategies that include encryption, firewalls, intrusion detection systems, and multi-factor authentication (MFA). Implementing Zero Trust Architecture (ZTA)where no user or system is automatically trusted—has become a key approach to strengthening security in highly interconnected environments.

Data Privacy and Regulatory Compliance

 In response to growing concerns over data misuse, governments worldwide have implemented strict data protection regulations. The General Data Protection Regulation (GDPR), enacted by the European Union, mandates that organizations handle personal data with transparency, security, and user consent. Similar laws, such as California's Consumer Privacy Act (CCPA) and Nigeria's Data Protection Regulation (NDPR), aim to enhance individual privacy rights while holding companies accountable for their data practices.

Despite regulatory efforts, challenges remain in enforcing data privacy laws globally, as digital data often transcends national boundaries. The emergence of decentralized identity solutions and privacy-preserving technologies, such as homomorphic encryption and differential privacy, may offer innovative ways to enhance data security while ensuring compliance with privacy regulations.

As data continues to fuel innovation, the ability to balance security, privacy, and usability will be a defining factor in maintaining trust in the digital economy.

The Digital Divide and Accessibility: Bridging the Gap in the Digital Age

While technological advancements have brought about unprecedented levels of connectivity, they have also exposed and, in some cases, widened the digital divide—the gap between those with access to digital technologies and those without. The divide is influenced by factors such as geographical location, socioeconomic status, education level, and infrastructure availability.

Challenges in Accessing Digital Technologies

Many rural and underdeveloped regions lack basic internet connectivity, preventing residents from accessing online education, remote work opportunities, and e-commerce platforms. In some cases, even urban areas experience disparities, as high-speed broadband remains unaffordable for low-income households. The lack of access to smart devices, digital payment systems, and cloud-based applications further exacerbates inequality in participation within the digital economy.

Beyond infrastructure, the lack of digital literacy remains a significant barrier. Many individuals, especially in older generations or developing economies, lack the necessary skills to navigate digital tools effectively. This limits their ability to benefit from online banking, healthcare services, and educational resources, further deepening economic disparities.

Strategies for Closing the Digital Divide

Governments, businesses, and non-profit organizations are actively working to close the digital gap by investing in affordable internet access, expanding mobile network coverage, and promoting digital literacy programs. Initiatives like Google's Project Loon, which deploys high-altitude balloons to provide internet access in remote areas, and Facebook's Free Basics, which offers free access to essential online services, aim to bring connectivity to underserved populations.

Additionally, public-private partnerships are playing a key role in expanding internet accessibility. Governments are collaborating with technology firms to deploy fiber-optic networks, improve satellite-based internet coverage, and establish community digital centers that provide free training and access to computing resources.

Digital Inclusion and Economic Growth

Bridging the digital divide is not just a matter of social equity; it is also essential for economic growth and innovation. Increased internet penetration and digital literacy drive job creation, entrepreneurship, and access to global markets. Digital inclusion empowers individuals to participate in e-learning, telemedicine, and online commerce, ultimately fostering a more inclusive, connected, and digitally fluent society.

Efforts to make technology more accessible must continue, ensuring that no one is left behind in an increasingly digital world.

The Future of Data Flow and Interconnectivity: Emerging Technologies and Their Impact

As technological innovation accelerates, the way data is generated, transmitted, and utilized will undergo profound transformations. Emerging technologies such as 5G networks, artificial intelligence (AI), quantum computing, and blockchain are poised to redefine the digital landscape, enhancing connectivity, processing capabilities, and security. The rollout of 5G technology promises ultra-fast data transmission speeds, ultra-low latency, and increased network capacity. Unlike previous generations of mobile networks, 5G enables real-time communication between billions of connected devices, powering applications such as autonomous vehicles, smart cities, and industrial automation.

With 5G, industries will experience enhanced IoT capabilities, enabling seamless machine-to-machine communication and real-time analytics. Smart grids, remote surgery, and augmented reality (AR) applications will become more viable as network reliability and speed reach new heights. However, concerns about 5G infrastructure costs, cybersecurity risks, and geopolitical tensions surrounding its deployment remain key challenges to address.

Artificial Intelligence and Data-Driven Decision-Making

AI and machine learning algorithms are revolutionizing data flow by automating complex decision-making processes, optimizing business operations, and enabling predictive analytics. AI-powered chatbots, recommendation systems, and fraud detection tools are already transforming industries such as healthcare, finance, and retail.

As AI continues to evolve, it will play a crucial role in managing data congestion, optimizing traffic routing, and detecting cyber threats in real-time. However, issues surrounding AI bias, ethical concerns, and data privacy must be carefully addressed to ensure responsible AI deployment.

Quantum Computing and the Future of Data Security

Quantum computing represents a paradigm shift in data processing, with the potential to solve problems exponentially faster than classical computers. This technology is expected to revolutionize fields such as cryptography, materials science, and complex simulations.

One of the most significant implications of quantum computing is its impact on cybersecurity. Current encryption methods, such as RSA and AES, rely on mathematical complexity to secure data. Quantum computers, however, could break traditional encryption protocols in minutes, prompting the need for post-quantum cryptography—new security methods resistant to quantum attacks.

Despite its promise, quantum computing is still in its early stages, with challenges related to scalability, stability, and hardware development. Continued research and investment in this field will determine how soon its full potential can be realized.

Blockchain and Decentralized Data Management

Blockchain technology is emerging as a solution for secure and transparent data management. By leveraging decentralized ledgers, blockchain ensures tamper-proof transactions, secure identity verification, and decentralized cloud storage.

Blockchain applications are expanding beyond cryptocurrencies, with potential use cases in healthcare record management, supply chain transparency, and smart contracts. As blockchain adoption grows, it could revolutionize data governance by eliminating intermediaries, reducing fraud, and enhancing data integrity. The trajectory of data flow and interconnectivity will be shaped by technological advancements and the ability to navigate security, ethical, and accessibility challenges. Collaboration between governments, tech companies, and regulatory bodies will be crucial in ensuring that data-driven innovations contribute to a more efficient, secure, and inclusive digital future.

By investing in secure infrastructure, digital inclusion, and emerging technologies, societies can harness the full potential of data to create a world where connectivity empowers individuals, businesses thrive, and information is safeguarded for generations to come.

CHAPTER FIVE

ARTIFICIAL INTELLIGENCE AND MACHINE LEARNING NAVIGATING THE FUTURE

Artificial intelligence (AI) and machine learning (ML) have evolved into foundational pillars of modern society, profoundly impacting industries, economies, and the way people interact with technology in their everyday lives. These advanced technologies are driving innovation across a wide range of sectors, from healthcare and finance to transportation and entertainment. Self-driving cars, for instance, are revolutionizing the automotive industry by enhancing safety and efficiency, while AI-powered personalized recommendations are transforming how consumers discover products, services, and content. Beyond these visible applications, AI and ML are also enabling breakthroughs in areas such as natural language processing, robotics, and predictive analytics, empowering businesses, and individuals to make smarter, data-driven decisions. As these technologies continue to advance, they are not only reshaping existing systems but also creating entirely new possibilities, paving the way for a future where intelligent systems seamlessly integrate into every aspect of human life. The growing influence of AI and ML underscores their significance as key drivers of progress in the 21st century, with the potential to address complex global challenges and improve quality of life on an unprecedented scale.

Artificial intelligence refers to the simulation of human intelligence in machines, enabling them to perform tasks that typically require cognitive functions such as reasoning, learning, problem-solving, perception, and language understanding. AI systems are designed to process vast amounts of data, recognize patterns, and make informed decisions, often with minimal human intervention. AI encompasses various subfields, including natural language processing (NLP), computer vision, robotics, and expert systems. The goal of AI is to develop machines that can automate repetitive tasks, enhance efficiency, and solve complex problems across multiple domains. The effectiveness of AI depends on algorithms, computational power, and the quality of data used for training models. The evolution of AI has been driven by advancements in deep learning, neural networks, and data analytics. These innovations allow AI systems to continuously improve their performance, adapt to new inputs, and execute functions with increasing precision.

Machine learning is a subset of AI that focuses on building algorithms that enable computers to learn from data and improve their performance over time without being explicitly programmed. Unlike traditional rule-based programming, where predefined instructions dictate every possible outcome, ML models identify patterns in data and make predictions or decisions based on their findings.

The distinction between AI and ML lies in their scope. AI encompasses a broader concept of intelligent systems, including both rule-based and learning-based approaches. ML, on the other hand, is specifically concerned with the development of statistical models and algorithms that allow computers to "learn" from past experiences.

Machine learning operates by processing large datasets, identifying correlations, and adjusting its decision-making criteria to optimize accuracy. The learning process involves training models on labeled or unlabeled data, evaluating their performance, and refining them to minimize errors. The success of ML models depends on data quality, computational power, and algorithmic efficiency.

What is machine learning? How it Differs from AI and How Machines "Learn"

Machine learning is a subset of AI that focuses on building algorithms that enable computers to learn from data and improve their performance over time without being explicitly programmed. Unlike traditional rule-based programming, where predefined instructions dictate every possible outcome, ML models identify patterns in data and make predictions or decisions based on their findings.

The distinction between AI and ML lies in their scope. AI encompasses a broader concept of intelligent systems, including both rule-based and learning-based approaches. ML, on the other hand, is specifically concerned with the development of statistical models and algorithms that allow computers to "learn" from past experiences.

Machine learning operates by processing large datasets, identifying correlations, and adjusting its decision-making criteria to optimize accuracy. The learning process involves training models on labeled or unlabeled data, evaluating their performance, and refining them to minimize errors. The success of ML models depends on data quality, computational power, and algorithmic efficiency.

Types of AI

AI is often categorized into different levels based on its capabilities, ranging from narrowly focused systems to highly advanced, theoretical constructs that surpass human intelligence.

Narrow AI (Weak AI)

Narrow AI refers to AI systems designed to perform specific tasks within a limited domain. These systems do not possess general intelligence or self-awareness but excel in predefined functions. Examples of Narrow AI include virtual assistants like Siri and Google Assistant, recommendation algorithms used by Netflix and Amazon, and AI-powered fraud detection systems in banking.

Narrow AI relies on machine learning and deep learning techniques to process data, recognize patterns, and generate insights. Despite its impressive capabilities, it lacks the ability to think, reason, or transfer knowledge across different domains.

General AI (Strong AI)

General AI represents a theoretical form of artificial intelligence that possesses human-like cognitive abilities, including reasoning, learning, problem-solving, and adaptability across multiple domains. Unlike Narrow AI, which is confined to specific tasks,

General AI would be capable of performing any intellectual task that a human can do.

The development of General AI remains a distant goal, as current AI systems lack self-awareness, emotional intelligence, and the ability to generalize knowledge beyond their training data. Achieving general AI would require breakthroughs in machine consciousness, reasoning, and autonomous decision-making.

Super AI (Artificial Superintelligence)

Super AI is a speculative concept referring to AI systems that surpass human intelligence in all aspects, including creativity, emotional intelligence, and problem-solving. Super AI would be capable of outperforming the best human minds in scientific discovery, artistic expression, and strategic thinking.

The idea of super AI raises ethical and existential concerns, as such an entity could potentially surpass human control. Scientists and philosophers have debated the implications of developing a superintelligent system, emphasizing the need for safeguards, ethical considerations, and regulatory frameworks to ensure that AI advancements remain beneficial to humanity.

Machine learning models learn from data through different approaches, each tailored to specific types of problems and available datasets. The three primary learning paradigms in ML are supervised learning, unsupervised learning, and reinforcement learning.

Supervised Learning

Supervised learning involves training an AI model using labeled datasets, where input data is paired with the correct output. The model learns by analyzing these labeled examples and identifying patterns to make predictions on new, unseen data.

This approach is widely used in applications such as spam email detection, medical diagnosis, and facial recognition. Common algorithms in supervised learning include decision trees, support vector machines (SVMs), and neural networks. The success of supervised learning depends on the availability of high-quality labeled data, which can be time-consuming and expensive to collect.

Unsupervised Learning

Unsupervised learning involves training models on unlabeled data, meaning the system must discover patterns and relationships without predefined outputs. The goal is to identify hidden structures, correlations, or clusters within the data.

This approach is commonly used for customer segmentation, anomaly detection, and recommendation systems. Techniques such as clustering (e.g., K-means clustering) and dimensionality reduction (e.g., principal component analysis) are widely used in unsupervised learning. Unlike supervised learning, this method does not require labeled data, making it suitable for scenarios where labeling is impractical or costly.

Reinforcement Learning

Reinforcement learning (RL) is a dynamic learning process in which an AI agent interacts with an environment, receiving rewards or penalties based on its actions. The goal of the agent is to maximize cumulative rewards over time by learning the best strategies through trial and error.

This approach is particularly effective in decision-making problems where sequential actions impact future outcomes. Reinforcement learning is used in robotics, game-playing AI (such as AlphaGo and OpenAI's Dota 2 bot), and autonomous vehicle navigation. RL algorithms, such as Q-learning and Deep Q Networks (DQNs), enable AI agents to learn optimal strategies in complex environments.

The distinction between Narrow AI, General AI, and Super AI highlights the varying levels of intelligence and autonomy AI systems can achieve, with General AI and Super AI remaining speculative goals for the future. Machine learning models learn through different paradigms—supervised, unsupervised, and reinforcement learning—each offering unique benefits and applications.

As AI and ML technologies advance, ethical considerations, security concerns, and regulatory frameworks will play crucial roles in shaping their development. The future of AI holds immense potential, promising innovations that could redefine industries, enhance human capabilities, and push the boundaries of what machines can achieve.

The Impact of AI and ML on Society

Artificial intelligence (AI) and machine learning (ML) have fundamentally altered the landscape of numerous sectors, redefining how organizations function and profoundly influencing daily life. By harnessing the power of these technologies, businesses can automate processes, boost productivity, and uncover valuable insights that fuel groundbreaking advancements. Across fields such as healthcare, finance, education, transportation, and entertainment, AI and ML are unlocking opportunities that were once the realm of imagination, turning futuristic concepts into tangible realities. Their ability to analyze vast amounts of data, adapt to changing conditions, and deliver intelligent solutions is not only optimizing existing systems but also paving the way for entirely new paradigms, making them indispensable tools in shaping the modern world.

Healthcare: AI in Diagnosis, Robotic Surgeries, and Personalized Medicine

AI has made remarkable strides in the healthcare industry, improving diagnostic accuracy, optimizing treatment plans, and streamlining administrative processes. One of the most impactful applications is in medical imaging, where AI-powered systems analyze X-rays, MRIs, and CT scans to detect diseases such as cancer, neurological disorders, and cardiovascular conditions with high precision. These AI models, trained on vast datasets, can often identify abnormalities faster and more accurately than human radiologists, reducing diagnostic errors and enabling early intervention.

Robotic-assisted surgeries have also gained prominence, allowing surgeons to perform complex procedures with greater precision, minimal invasiveness, and reduced recovery times for patients. AI-powered robotic systems, such as the da Vinci Surgical System, enhance a surgeon's capabilities by providing real-time insights, stabilizing movements, and improving visualization of the surgical site.

Personalized medicine, another revolutionary advancement, leverages AI and ML to tailor treatments based on a patient's genetic makeup, lifestyle, and medical history. By analyzing vast amounts of genomic and clinical data, AI can help predict an individual's response to specific medications, optimizing drug selection and dosages for maximum efficacy. This approach enhances patient outcomes while minimizing side effects, marking a shift from generalized treatment plans to highly customized healthcare solutions.

Finance: Fraud Detection, AI-Driven Trading, and Risk Assessment

The financial sector has been a pioneer in adopting AI and ML to enhance security, optimize investment strategies, and improve customer experiences. One of the most critical applications is fraud detection, where AI algorithms analyze transaction patterns to identify suspicious activities in real time. By leveraging historical transaction data, AI-powered fraud detection systems can detect anomalies, flag potentially fraudulent transactions, and prevent financial crimes before they occur.

AI-driven trading has also revolutionized financial markets, with hedge funds and investment firms relying on machine learning algorithms to make data-driven trading decisions. These AI models analyze vast amounts of market data, detect trends, and execute high-frequency trades with remarkable speed and accuracy. By eliminating human biases and emotional decision-making, AI-driven trading systems enhance efficiency and profitability in stock markets.

Risk assessment and credit scoring have been improved through AI's ability to evaluate a borrower's creditworthiness based on alternative data sources beyond traditional credit scores. Machine learning models assess factors such as spending behavior, social media activity, and transaction history to make more accurate lending decisions. This enables financial institutions to extend credit to previously underserved populations while minimizing the risk of default.

Education: AI-Powered Tutoring, Automated Grading, and Adaptive Learning

AI and ML are transforming the education sector by personalizing learning experiences, automating administrative tasks, and improving accessibility for students of all backgrounds. AI-powered tutoring systems provide students with real-time assistance, answering questions, offering explanations, and guiding them through complex concepts. These virtual tutors, powered by natural language processing (NLP) and machine learning, enhance the learning experience by adapting to individual student needs.

Automated grading has also streamlined the assessment process, reducing the workload on educators and ensuring fair and unbiased evaluations. AI-based systems can grade multiple-choice exams, short-answer questions, and even essays using advanced NLP techniques. By analyzing student responses, these systems provide instant feedback, allowing learners to track their progress and improve their understanding of the subject matter.

Adaptive learning platforms leverage AI to tailor educational content based on a student's learning pace, strengths, and weaknesses. These platforms continuously analyze student performance and adjust lesson plans, accordingly, ensuring that learners receive personalized instruction. This approach enhances student engagement, improves retention rates, and bridges knowledge gaps more effectively than traditional one-size-fits-all teaching methods.

Transportation: Self-Driving Cars, Smart Traffic Management, and Logistics

AI and ML have significantly impacted the transportation industry, driving innovations in autonomous vehicles, traffic optimization, and logistics management. Self-driving cars, powered by AI algorithms and sensor technologies, aim to reduce human errors, improve road safety, and enhance mobility for individuals with disabilities or limited access to transportation. Companies like Tesla, Waymo, and Uber are leading the development of autonomous vehicles, utilizing deep learning models to interpret real-time data from cameras, LiDAR, and radar sensors.

Smart traffic management systems leverage AI to optimize traffic flow, reduce congestion, and improve urban mobility. By analyzing data from traffic cameras, GPS sensors, and connected vehicles, AI-powered systems can dynamically adjust traffic signals, reroute vehicles, and predict traffic patterns. These intelligent systems contribute to more efficient transportation networks, reducing travel times and minimizing fuel consumption.

Logistics and supply chain management have also benefited from AI-driven optimizations. Machine learning models analyze demand patterns, weather conditions, and transportation constraints to enhance route planning and inventory management. AI-powered logistics solutions enable companies to optimize delivery schedules, reduce operational costs, and improve supply chain resilience. The integration of AI in logistics has proven essential for e-commerce giants such as Amazon, which use AI-driven robots and predictive analytics to streamline warehouse operations and enhance last-mile delivery.

Entertainment: AI-Generated Music, Deepfake Technology, and Recommendation Engines

The entertainment industry has embraced AI and ML to revolutionize content creation, audience engagement, and media distribution. AI-generated music has emerged as a novel creative tool, enabling composers and producers to experiment with new sounds and styles. AI-driven platforms like OpenAI's MuseNet and Google's Magenta use deep learning models to compose original pieces, blending multiple genres and generating melodies that rival human compositions.

Deepfake technology, while controversial, has demonstrated AI's ability to manipulate audio and video content with astonishing realism. Using generative adversarial networks (GANs), deepfake AI can create hyper-realistic digital alterations, allowing actors to be digitally resurrected, scenes to be reimagined, and historical footage to be enhanced. While this technology has been used in entertainment and film production, it also raises ethical concerns regarding misinformation and digital identity fraud.

Recommendation engines powered by AI have transformed how audiences consume content. Streaming services like Netflix, Spotify, and YouTube leverage machine learning algorithms to analyze user preferences and suggest personalized content. These AI-driven recommendations enhance user experiences by curating content tailored to individual tastes, increasing engagement, and optimizing content delivery.

AI and ML have ushered in a new era of technological advancements that continue to reshape industries and redefine human experiences. In healthcare, AI enhances diagnostics, robotic surgeries, and personalized treatments. In finance, it strengthens fraud detection, optimizes trading strategies, and improves risk assessment. Education benefits from AI-powered tutoring, automated grading, and adaptive learning, ensuring personalized instruction for students. Transportation is evolving with self-driving cars, smart traffic management, and AI-driven logistics. Meanwhile, entertainment has seen remarkable innovations through AI-generated music, deepfake technology, and intelligent recommendation engines.

As AI and ML technologies continue to advance, their impact on society will expand further, offering new opportunities while also presenting ethical and regulatory challenges. Striking a balance between innovation and responsible AI deployment will be crucial to ensuring that these transformative technologies benefit humanity while mitigating potential risks.

Challenges and Ethical Considerations in AI

As artificial intelligence (AI) becomes increasingly integrated into daily life, its transformative potential is accompanied by significant challenges and ethical dilemmas. The development and deployment of AI raise concerns related to bias, job displacement, data privacy, decision-making, and its potential role in military applications. These issues require careful examination to ensure that AI technologies are implemented in ways that are fair, responsible, and beneficial to society as a whole.

Bias in AI: How AI Can Inherit Human Prejudices from Data

One of the most critical ethical challenges in AI is bias, which occurs when AI systems reflect and perpetuate human prejudices embedded in the data they are trained on. AI models learn from vast amounts of historical data, and if that data contains biases related to gender, race, socioeconomic status, or other factors, the AI can unintentionally reinforce these biases in its decisions and predictions.

For example, biased hiring algorithms have been found to favor male candidates over female ones due to historical hiring trends in certain industries. Similarly, facial recognition systems have been shown to misidentify people of color at higher rates than white individuals, leading to potential injustices in law enforcement and security applications. AI-driven credit scoring and lending systems have also exhibited bias, disproportionately denying loans to minority groups based on historical financial data.

Addressing bias in AI requires a multifaceted approach that includes using diverse and representative datasets, implementing fairness-aware algorithms, and conducting rigorous audits to detect and mitigate bias. Transparency in AI development and the involvement of ethicists, social scientists, and impacted communities in AI governance can help ensure that AI systems do not exacerbate existing social inequalities.

Job Displacement: Will AI Replace Human Jobs or Create New Opportunities?

The rise of AI-driven automation has sparked widespread concerns about job displacement, particularly in industries where routine tasks can be efficiently performed by machines. Manufacturing, retail, customer service, and even white-collar professions such as accounting and legal research are increasingly seeing AI-powered systems take over tasks traditionally done by humans.

Automation has already led to significant job losses in industries such as manufacturing, where robotic systems now handle assembly-line work with greater efficiency and precision than human workers. In retail, self-checkout kiosks and AI-powered chatbots are replacing cashiers and customer service representatives, reducing labor costs for businesses. Even in professional fields like journalism, AI-generated news articles and automated content summarization are challenging traditional roles.

However, AI is also creating new job opportunities, particularly in areas such as AI development, data science, and cybersecurity. The demand for AI specialists, machine learning engineers, and AI ethics consultants is rising, leading to the emergence of new career paths. Additionally, AI is augmenting human capabilities rather than outright replacing workers in many fields. For instance, in healthcare, AI assists doctors in diagnosing diseases and analyzing medical data, allowing them to focus on patient care rather than administrative tasks.

The key to addressing job displacement lies in reskilling and upskilling the workforce. Governments, businesses, and educational institutions must invest in training programs to help workers transition into AI-related roles or industries where human skills such as creativity, emotional intelligence, and complex problem-solving remain irreplaceable.

Data Privacy and Security: AI's Role in Surveillance and Personal Data Usage

AI's ability to analyze vast amounts of personal data raises concerns about privacy and security, particularly in an era where data collection is ubiquitous. Many AI applications, from social media algorithms to smart home devices and facial recognition technology, rely on personal data to function effectively. However, this extensive data collection poses risks related to surveillance, unauthorized data usage, and breaches of individual privacy.

Governments and corporations use AI-driven surveillance systems to monitor citizens, track behaviors, and predict potential security threats. While these systems can enhance public safety, they also raise ethical questions about mass surveillance and the erosion of personal freedoms. In authoritarian regimes, AI-powered surveillance has been used to suppress dissent and control populations, leading to significant human rights concerns.

Data security is another major challenge, as AI systems are often targets of cyberattacks. Hackers can manipulate AI models through adversarial attacks, feeding them misleading data to trick them into making incorrect decisions. Additionally, large-scale data breaches expose sensitive user information, putting individuals at risk of identity theft and financial fraud.

To address these concerns, robust data protection regulations such as the General Data Protection Regulation (GDPR) and California Consumer Privacy Act (CCPA) have been implemented to give individuals greater control over their personal data. Companies developing AI systems must prioritize transparency, user consent, and ethical data handling practices to build trust and mitigate privacy risks.

AI and Decision-Making: The Risks of Over-Reliance on AI

AI is increasingly being used to make decisions in areas such as healthcare, criminal justice, hiring, and finance. While AI can process vast amounts of data and detect patterns that humans may overlook, over-reliance on AI can lead to flawed and unjust outcomes. AI-driven decision-making systems are fallible, and errors can have significant consequences, particularly when they impact people's lives and livelihoods.

In the legal system, predictive policing algorithms have been criticized for disproportionately targeting marginalized communities, reinforcing existing biases in law enforcement. In hiring, automatic resume screening tools may unintentionally exclude qualified candidates due to biased training data. In healthcare, AI-based diagnostic tools, while highly effective, may not always account for rare medical conditions or unique patient histories, leading to misdiagnoses.

Another risk of over-reliance on AI is the loss of human oversight. When organizations delegate critical decisions entirely to AI, they risk becoming blind to the system's limitations. Ethical decision-making often requires human judgment, empathy, and contextual understanding—qualities that AI lacks.

To mitigate these risks, AI should be used as a decision-support tool rather than a sole decision-maker. Human oversight is essential to ensure fairness, accountability, and ethical considerations in AI-driven processes. Organizations must also implement mechanisms for AI explainability, ensuring that AI-generated decisions can be interpreted, questioned, and corrected when necessary.

Autonomous Weapons and AI in Warfare: Ethical Dilemmas of AI in Military Applications

One of the most controversial applications of AI is its role in warfare and autonomous weapons. AI-powered military systems, including drones, surveillance tools, and autonomous weapons, have the potential to change the nature of warfare by reducing the need for human soldiers on the battlefield. While AI-driven military technology can improve precision and minimize collateral damage, it also raises profound ethical and moral questions.

The use of autonomous weapons—machines that can select and engage targets without human intervention—poses a significant threat to international security. If AI-controlled weapons make life-or-death decisions without human oversight, there is a risk of unintended casualties, wrongful attacks, and escalation of conflicts. The lack of accountability for autonomous weapons also raises concerns about war crimes and violations of humanitarian laws.

There are also fears that AI in warfare could lead to an arms race, with countries competing to develop increasingly sophisticated autonomous weapons. This could lower the threshold for conflict, as nations may be more willing to engage in military actions when AI-driven systems handle combat instead of human soldiers.

International discussions on AI in warfare are ongoing, with organizations such as the United Nations calling for regulations on autonomous weapons. Ethical AI development in military applications must ensure that human control remains integral to decision-making processes and that AI is used in ways that align with international humanitarian laws.

While AI offers immense potential to improve efficiency, decision-making, and automation, its development and deployment must be approached with ethical responsibility. Addressing bias, job displacement, data privacy, AI-driven decision-making, and military applications requires collaboration between governments, businesses, researchers, and ethicists. Transparent AI governance, ethical regulations, and ongoing public discourse will be essential in ensuring that AI serves humanity's best interests while minimizing potential risks and harms.

CHAPTER SIX

EXPLORING THE DEPTHS DATA MINING AND ANALYSIS TECHNIQUES

The concept of data mining has evolved significantly over the years. Traditionally, data analysis was based on statistical methods such as regression analysis, correlation studies, and hypothesis testing. These techniques required human expertise to manually examine datasets and identify meaningful patterns. As computing power increased, more advanced algorithms, such as clustering and classification models, were introduced, allowing for greater automation in pattern discovery.

With the rise of artificial intelligence and machine learning, data mining has reached new levels of sophistication. AI-driven analytics can process vast amounts of structured and unstructured data at unprecedented speeds, identifying trends and correlations that human analysts might overlook. Deep learning models, natural language processing, and neural networks have further enhanced the capabilities of data mining, enabling more accurate predictions and real-time insights. Today, businesses rely on AI-powered data mining to personalize customer experiences, detect fraudulent activities, and optimize supply chain management.

Difference Between Data Mining and Data Analysis: Discovering Patterns vs. Interpreting Data

While data mining and data analysis are closely related, they serve distinct purposes. Data mining focuses on discovering hidden patterns, relationships, and trends within large datasets. It involves applying algorithms and machine learning techniques to find correlations that may not be immediately obvious. The goal of data mining is to reveal insights that can drive decision-making and predictive modeling.

Data analysis, on the other hand, involves interpreting, summarizing, and presenting data to derive meaningful conclusions. It often relies on visualization techniques, statistical summaries, and descriptive analytics to help organizations understand past and current trends. While data mining uncovers the "what" and "how" behind data patterns, data analysis answers the "why," providing context and explanations for the observed patterns. In practice, data mining and data analysis often work together, with mining identifying patterns and analysis providing the insights needed to act on them.

Key Stages of Data Mining

1. Data Collection

The first step in data mining is gathering relevant data from various sources. Data can come from transactional databases, social media interactions, customer feedback, IoT sensors, financial records, and more. The quality of data collected plays a crucial role in the effectiveness of data mining, as incomplete or irrelevant data can lead to inaccurate insights. Organizations must ensure they collect data that is comprehensive, representative, and aligned with their objectives.

2. Data Cleaning and Preprocessing

Before data can be analyzed, it must be cleaned and prepared for processing. Raw data often contains errors, missing values, duplicate records, and inconsistencies that can affect the accuracy of data mining results. Data cleaning involves identifying and correcting these issues to improve data quality. Preprocessing techniques such as normalization, transformation, and feature selection are also applied to standardize the data and make it suitable for analysis.

In this stage, businesses may also integrate data from multiple sources to create a unified dataset. This step is crucial because poor data quality can lead to misleading patterns and incorrect conclusions. Effective preprocessing ensures that the data is reliable and ready for meaningful exploration.

3. Pattern Discovery

Once the data is cleaned and preprocessed, data mining techniques are applied to identify patterns, correlations, and trends. Various algorithms are used depending on the objectives of the analysis.

Classification assigns data points to predefined categories, often used in spam detection and medical diagnosis.

Clustering groups similar data points together without predefined labels, useful for market segmentation and anomaly detection.

Association Rule Mining identifies relationships between different variables, commonly used in market basket analysis (e.g., customers who buy bread often buy butter).

Regression analysis predicts numerical values based on past trends, useful for stock market predictions and sales forecasting.

Anomaly detection identifies outliers in data, often used in fraud detection and cybersecurity monitoring.

This stage is where the true power of data mining emerges, as these patterns provide actionable insights that can drive business strategies and operational improvements.

4. Interpretation and Decision-Making

The final stage of data mining involves interpreting the discovered patterns and using them to make informed decisions. Visualization tools such as graphs, heat maps, and dashboards help analysts and decision-makers understand the findings. The insights gained from data mining are then applied to solve business problems, optimize processes, and improve decision-making.

For example, in retail, data mining can help businesses predict customer purchasing behavior and optimize inventory management. In finance, banks use data mining to detect fraudulent transactions and assess credit risk. In healthcare, data mining aids in disease prediction and personalized treatment plans. The ability to turn raw data into actionable intelligence is what makes data mining such a powerful tool in the modern digital landscape. Data mining has transformed how organizations extract value from large datasets. From its roots in statistical analysis to the modern AI-driven approaches, data mining has become an essential tool for discovering hidden patterns and making data-driven decisions. By understanding its key stages—data collection, cleaning, pattern discovery, and interpretation—businesses can unlock valuable insights, improve efficiency, and gain a competitive edge in their respective industries. However, as data mining continues to evolve, ethical considerations such as privacy, bias, and data security must also be addressed to ensure responsible and fair use of data.

Core Data Mining Techniques

Classification is a fundamental data mining technique that involves categorizing data into predefined groups based on historical patterns. This technique is widely used in various industries to automate decision-making and improve predictive accuracy. One of the most common uses of classification is spam detection in emails. By analyzing email content and metadata, classification algorithms can identify whether an email is spam or not. In the medical field, classification is used for diagnosing diseases based on patient symptoms and medical records. Financial institutions use classification for credit scoring to assess a borrower's creditworthiness. Several techniques enable effective classification. Decision trees create a flowchart-like structure where each node represents a decision based on input features. Naïve Bayes, based on probability theory, is particularly effective for text classification tasks like spam filtering. Support Vector Machines (SVM) are powerful in high-dimensional spaces, making them useful for complex classification tasks such as image recognition and bioinformatics.

Clustering involves grouping similar data points together without predefined labels. This technique is particularly useful when discovering underlying patterns in large datasets.

Applications for Clustering

Businesses use clustering for customer segmentation, grouping customers based on purchasing behavior, demographics, or preferences to enhance marketing strategies. Fraud detection also benefits from clustering, as unusual patterns in financial transactions can indicate fraudulent activities. In genomics, clustering helps in DNA sequence analysis, identifying genetic similarities and differences.

Popular clustering techniques include K-means clustering, which partitions data into K clusters based on feature similarity. Hierarchical clustering builds a tree-like structure of nested clusters, useful for understanding relationships among data points. DBSCAN (density-based spatial clustering of applications with noise) is effective for detecting clusters of varying densities and identifying outliers.

Association rule learning helps uncover relationships between variables in large datasets. This technique is essential for market basket analysis and recommendation systems.

Applications of Association Rule Learning

Retailers leverage association rule learning to determine which products are frequently bought together. For example, if customers who buy bread also purchase butter, retailers can optimize product placement and cross-selling strategies. Online recommendation systems, such as those used by e-commerce platforms, rely on association rules to suggest relevant products based on user behavior.

The apriori algorithm systematically identifies frequent item sets and derives association rules. The FP-Growth Algorithm enhances efficiency by using a tree structure to mine patterns without generating candidate sets.

Anomaly detection identifies data points that significantly deviate from normal patterns, making it crucial for fraud detection, cybersecurity, and quality control.

Applications for Anomaly Detection

Banks use anomaly detection to detect fraudulent transactions by identifying unusual spending behaviors. Network security systems rely on anomaly detection to recognize potential cyber threats, such as unauthorized access or malware activity. In manufacturing, this technique helps identify defective products in quality control processes.

Isolation Forest is an effective technique that isolates anomalies by constructing decision trees and analyzing how quickly an observation becomes isolated. Local Outlier Factor (LOF) detects anomalies by comparing the local density of data points, flagging those that deviate significantly from their neighbors.

Regression analysis is a statistical technique used to predict continuous outcomes based on input variables. It is widely used in finance, marketing, and scientific research.

Applications for Regression Analysis

Financial analysts use regression analysis to predict stock prices based on historical trends. In sales forecasting, businesses rely on regression models to estimate future revenue based on factors such as seasonality and economic conditions. Climate scientists use regression to model temperature variations and predict future climate patterns.

Linear regression is the simplest form, establishing a linear relationship between dependent and independent variables. Polynomial regression extends this by fitting non-linear data trends. Ridge regression addresses multicollinearity by adding a penalty to regression coefficients, improving model stability.

Dimensionality reduction simplifies complex data while preserving essential information, making it useful for visualization, noise reduction, and efficiency improvement in machine learning models.

Applications for Dimensionality Reduction

Image compression benefits from dimensionality reduction techniques by reducing the storage size of images while maintaining visual quality. Text analysis leverages dimensionality reduction to remove redundant information and extract meaningful features from large text corpora. In machine learning, dimensionality reduction helps improve model performance by eliminating irrelevant features.

Principal Component Analysis (PCA) transforms data into a set of uncorrelated variables, capturing the most variance in fewer dimensions. t-Distributed Stochastic Neighbor Embedding (t-SNE) is effective for visualizing high-dimensional data by reducing it to two or three dimensions. Autoencoders, a type of neural network, learn efficient data representations, making them useful for noise reduction and feature extraction. Association rule learning uncovers relationships between variables, anomaly detection identifies outliers, regression analysis predicts continuous outcomes, and dimensionality reduction simplifies complex data. Understanding these techniques enables businesses and researchers to make informed decisions, optimize operations, and drive innovation in various domains.

Data Analysis Techniques: Understanding and Application

Data analysis is essential for making informed decisions, as it goes beyond simply collecting and mining data. It involves interpreting data to extract meaningful insights, recognizing patterns, and driving strategic actions. Various types of data analysis serve different purposes, ranging from summarizing past trends to making future predictions and recommending the best course of action.

Descriptive Analytics: Understanding Past Data

Descriptive analytics focuses on summarizing historical data to identify trends and patterns. It helps businesses and organizations gain insights into past performance by aggregating raw data into meaningful summaries. This type of analysis is commonly used in reports, dashboards, and business intelligence tools. For example, a retail company may analyze sales data over the past year to identify seasonal trends, while a social media manager may review engagement metrics to understand audience behavior. By presenting data in an understandable format—such as charts, graphs, and summaries, descriptive analytics provides the foundation for more advanced analyses.

Diagnostic Analytics: Explaining the Reasons Behind Events

While descriptive analytics tells what happened, diagnostic analytics explains why it happened. This type of analysis focuses on understanding relationships between different variables to determine the causes of specific outcomes. Common techniques include correlation analysis, regression analysis, and root cause analysis. For instance, if an e-commerce business notices a sudden drop in website traffic, diagnostic analytics can help determine whether it was due to a technical issue, a change in marketing strategy, or external factors such as a competitor's promotion. Businesses use diagnostic analytics to troubleshoot problems, refine strategies, and improve decision-making.

Predictive Analytics: Forecasting Future Trends

Predictive analytics leverages statistical models, machine learning algorithms, and historical data to make predictions about future events. By analyzing patterns in past data, predictive models can estimate likely outcomes, allowing businesses to plan ahead. This type of analysis is widely used in various industries, such as finance for credit scoring, healthcare for disease prediction, and retail for demand forecasting. For example, an airline may use predictive analytics to anticipate peak travel seasons and adjust ticket prices accordingly. Though not always 100% accurate, predictive analytics helps organizations make more informed decisions by providing data-driven foresight.

Prescriptive Analytics: Recommending the Best Course of Action

Prescriptive analytics takes predictive analytics a step further by suggesting specific actions to optimize outcomes. It combines machine learning, optimization algorithms, and business rules to determine the best possible decision in a given situation. This type of analysis is commonly used in recommendation systems, supply chain management, and automated decision-making. For example, streaming platforms like Netflix use prescriptive analytics to recommend movies and shows based on user preferences, while ride-hailing services like Uber suggest optimal pricing strategies during peak hours. By analyzing multiple scenarios and their potential impacts, predictive analytics helps businesses maximize efficiency and profitability.

Each type of data analysis serves a unique purpose, from understanding past trends to predicting future outcomes and recommending actions. Organizations that effectively integrate these analytical techniques gain a competitive advantage by making data-driven decisions that enhance performance and efficiency. As businesses continue to collect and store vast amounts of data, leveraging the right analytical approach is crucial for turning information into actionable insights.

Tools for Data Mining and Analysis

Several tools and programming languages assist data scientists in performing data mining and analysis. These tools are essential for handling structured and unstructured data, performing statistical computations, and visualizing insights for decision-making.

Programming Languages for Data Analysis

Python is one of the most widely used programming languages for data mining and analysis. Its popularity stems from its rich ecosystem of libraries, including Pandas for data manipulation, NumPy for numerical computations, Scikit-learn for machine learning, and TensorFlow for deep learning applications. Python's flexibility and readability make it a top choice for both beginners and experts in the field.

R is another powerful language, particularly favored for statistical analysis and visualization. With packages such as ggplot2, dplyr, and caret, R excels in handling complex statistical modeling and data visualization tasks, making it a preferred tool for statisticians and researchers.

Database and Querying Tools

SQL is a fundamental tool for data retrieval and management. It allows users to query structured data from relational databases efficiently, making it indispensable for businesses that rely on large datasets. With capabilities like data aggregation, filtering, and joins, SQL enables analysts to extract meaningful insights from extensive databases.

MongoDB is a NoSQL database designed to handle unstructured data. Unlike traditional relational databases, it stores data in flexible JSON-like documents, making it ideal for working with dynamic and complex datasets that do not fit neatly into tabular formats.

Data Visualization Tools

Tableau and Power BI are leading tools for creating interactive dashboards and visual analytics. They enable users to transform raw data into compelling visual stories, helping businesses make data-driven decisions. Their drag-and-drop interfaces make it easy to generate charts, graphs, and reports without requiring extensive programming knowledge.

Matplotlib and Seaborn are Python libraries specifically designed for data visualization. Matplotlib provides comprehensive tools for creating static, animated, and interactive plots, while Seaborn builds on Matplotlib, offering aesthetically pleasing statistical visualizations with minimal code. These libraries are essential for exploring data patterns and trends.

Big Data and Cloud-Based Analytics Platforms

Apache Spark is a powerful open-source framework designed for large-scale data processing. It enables distributed computing, making it highly efficient for handling massive datasets across multiple nodes. With built-in support for machine learning, real-time data processing, and SQL queries, Apache Spark is a go-to tool for big data analytics.

Google Big Query and AWS Redshift are cloud-based data warehousing solutions that offer scalable and fast analytics capabilities. Google Big Query provides serverless, highly scalable analytics with built-in machine learning support, allowing users to run complex queries on large datasets quickly. AWS Redshift is Amazon's fully managed data warehouse, optimized for high-performance analytics with advanced compression and query optimization techniques. These cloud solutions empower businesses to analyze vast amounts of data without the need for heavy infrastructure investments.

Challenges in Data Mining and Analysis

Data mining and analysis play a crucial role in extracting valuable insights from vast amounts of information, but the process is not without its challenges. Organizations that rely on data-driven decision-making must navigate several obstacles, including data quality issues, computational scalability, privacy concerns, and the interpretability of complex models. Addressing these challenges is essential for ensuring accurate, ethical, and effective data-driven outcomes.

Data Quality Issues: The Impact of Incomplete and Noisy Data

One of the biggest challenges in data mining and analysis is ensuring high-quality data. Incomplete, inconsistent, or noisy data can significantly impact the accuracy of analytical models and decision-making processes. Missing values, duplicate records, and erroneous entries can lead to misleading results and incorrect insights. For instance, if a company's customer database contains outdated email addresses or inconsistent purchase histories, predictive models used for targeted marketing campaigns may fail to identify the right audience. Organizations must invest in robust data-cleaning techniques, such as data imputation and outlier detection, to improve data accuracy before analysis. Without high-quality data, even the most advanced analytics techniques can yield unreliable results.

Scalability: Managing Large and Complex Datasets

As organizations collect increasingly large amounts of data from multiple sources, processing and analyzing such vast datasets becomes a significant challenge. Traditional data mining algorithms and analytical models often struggle to scale efficiently, requiring extensive computational resources. The rise of big data has made it necessary to develop high-performance computing solutions, such as distributed computing and cloud-based storage, to handle complex datasets. Companies dealing with large-scale data analysis, such as social media platforms or financial institutions, must leverage scalable technologies like Hadoop, Spark, and parallel processing techniques to ensure fast and efficient data processing. Without proper scalability solutions, data analysis can become time-consuming and cost-prohibitive, limiting an organization's ability to derive timely insights.

Privacy Concerns: Ethical and Legal Implications of Data Use

With the growing use of personal and sensitive data in data mining, privacy has become a major concern. Organizations must navigate strict regulations, such as the General Data Protection Regulation (GDPR) and the Nigeria Data Protection Act, to ensure responsible data handling. Unauthorized access, data breaches, and unethical data usage can lead to legal consequences and damage public trust. For example, businesses that collect user data for personalized marketing must obtain consent and ensure data security to avoid violating privacy laws. Ethical concerns also arise when analyzing behavioral patterns, as companies may exploit personal information for financial gain without transparency. Implementing robust data governance frameworks, encryption methods, and strict access controls is crucial for maintaining compliance and protecting user privacy.

Algorithm Interpretability Understanding and Explaining Complex Models

As machine learning and artificial intelligence become more advanced, the complexity of analytical models has increased, making them difficult to interpret and explain. Many modern algorithms, such as deep learning neural networks, function as "black boxes," meaning their decision-making processes are not easily understood by humans. This lack of transparency can be problematic in critical applications, such as healthcare and finance, where decision-makers need clear explanations for predictive outcomes. For instance, if an AI-powered loan approval system denies a customer's application, the organization must be able to justify the decision to avoid bias and discrimination. To address this challenge, researchers and businesses are exploring explainable AI (XAI) techniques, such as SHAP values and LIME, which help break down complex models into interpretable components. Ensuring model transparency is essential for building trust, improving accountability, and making data-driven decisions more actionable. Despite its transformative potential, data mining and analysis come with significant challenges that must be addressed for successful implementation. High-quality data is the foundation of accurate analysis, while scalable computing solutions enable efficient processing of large datasets. Ethical data handling practices ensure compliance with privacy regulations, and model interpretability is crucial for trust and transparency. Organizations that proactively tackle these challenges can fully leverage data analytics to drive innovation, optimize operations, and enhance decision-making in an increasingly data-driven world.

CHAPTER SEVEN

SAFEGUARDING THE FRONTIERS DATA SECURITY AND PRIVACY

In an era where data is considered the new oil, safeguarding its integrity, confidentiality, and availability has become a global priority. From personal user information to corporate trade secrets and government intelligence, data is at the core of decision-making, innovation, and economic growth. However, with the increasing reliance on digital platforms and cloud-based infrastructures, the risks associated with cyber threats, data breaches, and privacy violations have escalated. This chapter delves into the multifaceted aspects of data security and privacy, exploring the evolving cyber threat landscape, regulatory frameworks, and the ethical dilemmas that arise in the pursuit of technological advancement.

The Evolving Landscape of Cyber Threats

The rapid evolution of technology has brought unparalleled convenience and connectivity, but it has also exposed organizations and individuals to an increasing array of cyber threats.

Cybercriminals continually develop more sophisticated techniques to exploit vulnerabilities in systems, often targeting businesses, financial institutions, and even government agencies. Ransomware, phishing, distributed denial-of-service (DDoS) attacks, and insider threats have all become prominent concerns in the cybersecurity landscape.

One of the most alarming trends in cyber threats is the rise of ransomware attacks. Malicious actors infiltrate systems, encrypt critical files, and demand ransom payments in exchange for restoring access. High-profile cases, such as the 2021 Colonial Pipeline attack, highlight the severe consequences of such incidents, causing disruptions in supply chains and significant financial losses. Organizations must implement robust defense mechanisms, such as endpoint security solutions, network segmentation, and continuous monitoring, to mitigate these threats.

Another prevalent cyber threat is data breaches, where sensitive information, including personally identifiable information (PII), financial records, and proprietary business data, is exposed to unauthorized entities. Companies such as Equifax, Facebook, and Marriott have experienced massive data breaches, affecting millions of customers worldwide. These incidents underscore the importance of encryption, secure authentication protocols, and employee training in reducing the likelihood of breaches.

Furthermore, phishing remains a common method used by attackers to deceive individuals into revealing confidential information. Social engineering tactics, such as impersonating trusted entities or creating fake websites, trick users into disclosing login credentials or downloading malware. The proliferation of artificial intelligence (AI) has further enhanced phishing tactics, making it more challenging to detect fraudulent attempts. Security awareness training and advanced email filtering mechanisms are crucial in minimizing phishing risks.

As cyber threats continue to evolve, businesses and governments must adopt proactive approaches to cybersecurity. Artificial intelligence and machine learning are increasingly being integrated into security frameworks to detect anomalies, identify suspicious patterns, and respond to potential threats in real time. The future of cybersecurity lies in automation, predictive analytics, and collaboration among cybersecurity experts to stay ahead of malicious actors.

Balancing Privacy and Innovation

While the digital revolution has unlocked immense opportunities for innovation, it has also raised significant concerns about data privacy. Organizations collect and analyze vast amounts of user data to enhance customer experiences, optimize services, and drive revenue growth. However, the ethical implications of data collection and usage remain a contentious issue, with concerns about surveillance, consent, and data ownership coming to the forefront.

The implementation of regulatory frameworks such as the General Data Protection Regulation (GDPR) in Europe and the California Consumer Privacy Act (CCPA) in the United States has set a precedent for data protection worldwide. These regulations enforce stringent guidelines on how businesses collect, store, and process user data. Companies must obtain explicit user consent before gathering personal information, provide transparency on data usage, and ensure that users have the right to request data deletion. Failure to comply with these regulations can result in hefty fines and reputational damage.

Despite these legal safeguards, data privacy remains a challenge in an interconnected world where smart devices, social media, and artificial intelligence are deeply embedded in everyday life. The rise of Internet of Things (IoT) devices, such as smart home assistants, wearable technology, and connected vehicles, has introduced new concerns about data security. These devices continuously collect data on user behavior, preferences, and interactions, raising questions about how this information is stored, shared, and protected.

Moreover, the increasing reliance on artificial intelligence and big data analytics has led to ethical dilemmas surrounding data privacy. AI algorithms process vast datasets to make predictions and recommendations, often without users fully understanding how their data is being utilized. Concerns over algorithmic bias, discrimination, and surveillance capitalism have sparked debates on whether organizations prioritize innovation at the expense of individual privacy rights.

To address these concerns, businesses must implement privacy-by-design principles, embedding security and ethical considerations into their technological innovations from the outset. Secure data encryption, anonymization techniques, and transparent data policies can help build trust with consumers and regulatory bodies. Additionally, organizations should empower users with greater control over their data, allowing them to customize privacy settings, opt-out of data sharing, and access clear disclosures on how their information is used.

The balance between privacy and innovation is a delicate one. While data-driven technologies have the potential to revolutionize industries, they must be developed and deployed with ethical responsibility. Companies that prioritize user trust and data protection will not only comply with legal requirements but also gain a competitive advantage in an increasingly privacy-conscious market.

The Future of Data Security and Privacy

As the digital landscape continues to evolve, the future of data security and privacy will be shaped by emerging technologies, regulatory advancements, and shifting consumer expectations. Quantum computing, blockchain, and decentralized identity solutions are poised to transform how data is secured and managed.

Quantum computing, while still in its infancy, has the potential to break traditional encryption methods, posing both a risk and an opportunity for cybersecurity. Researchers are actively working on quantum-resistant encryption techniques to prepare for this technological shift. Similarly, blockchain technology offers decentralized and tamper-proof data storage solutions, reducing the risk of unauthorized data modifications and breaches.

Meanwhile, decentralized identity models, where users have greater control over their digital identities without relying on centralized authorities, are gaining traction. This approach empowers individuals to manage their personal information securely while reducing the risks associated with data breaches.

Ultimately, data security and privacy will remain at the forefront of technological progress. Governments, businesses, and individuals must work together to establish a digital ecosystem that prioritizes both innovation and the protection of personal information. By embracing ethical data practices, adopting innovative security measures, and fostering a culture of cybersecurity awareness, society can navigate the complexities of the digital era while safeguarding the frontiers of data protection.

CHAPTER EIGHT

BUILDING BRIDGES DATA INTEGRATION AND INTEROPERABILITY

The digital world is built on data, yet its true power is realized only when information flows seamlessly across systems, organizations, and industries. Businesses, governments, and researchers depend on data integration to make informed decisions, drive innovation, and improve efficiency. However, the increasing complexity of data ecosystems has created challenges in achieving interoperability, with organizations struggling to merge structured and unstructured data from various sources.

This chapter explores the importance of data integration, the barriers posed by fragmented data systems, the role of standardized frameworks in achieving seamless interoperability, and the future of data-driven collaboration in a connected world. It also examines the impact of emerging technologies, such as artificial intelligence, blockchain, and cloud computing, on improving data sharing across industries. By building bridges between disparate data sources, organizations can unlock the full potential of information, leading to smarter decision-making, enhanced productivity, and more efficient services.

Overcoming the Challenges of Fragmented Data Systems

One of the biggest hurdles in achieving effective data integration is fragmentation. Data is often stored in multiple locations, across different formats, and managed by different software solutions that do not communicate with one another. This lack of connectivity results in inefficiencies, duplication of efforts, and inconsistencies in data analysis.

A major industry affected by data fragmentation is healthcare. Hospitals, clinics, and insurance companies operate on different electronic health record (EHR) systems, many of which do not share data seamlessly. This fragmentation means that when a patient visits a new provider, their medical history may be incomplete or inaccessible, leading to redundant tests, misdiagnoses, and inefficient treatment plans. For example, a patient may have undergone diagnostic tests at one hospital, but if their medical records are not integrated with another facility's system, they may have to repeat those tests—wasting time and resources.

Similarly, in financial services, banks, credit unions, and fintech startups store customer data in separate databases, making it difficult to provide seamless banking experiences. A customer applying for a loan might have a credit history scattered across multiple institutions, requiring manual verification processes that slow down approvals. Moreover, fragmented financial data creates vulnerabilities that fraudsters can exploit, as organizations struggle to cross-check transactional patterns in real-time.

The e-commerce and logistics sectors also suffer from fragmented data ecosystems. Online retailers rely on multiple platforms—such as payment gateways, inventory management systems, and customer relationship management (CRM) software—that may not be fully integrated. A lack of synchronization between these systems can lead to issues like overselling products, delayed shipments, and poor customer experiences. Logistics companies face similar challenges when tracking packages across different carriers, warehouses, and regions.

To address these fragmentation challenges, organizations must adopt data integration strategies that ensure seamless connectivity across platforms. Middleware solutions, such as enterprise service buses (ESBs) and data lakes, provide centralized repositories where information from multiple sources can be collected, cleaned, and processed. Application programming interfaces (APIs) allow software applications to communicate with one another, facilitating real-time data exchange. Additionally, cloud computing platforms enable businesses to integrate data stored on-premises with cloud-based services, improving scalability and accessibility.

However, data integration is not just about technology, it also requires addressing data governance issues such as data quality, consistency, and security. Poor data governance can lead to inaccuracies, redundancies, and compliance risks, making it difficult for organizations to derive meaningful insights. By implementing data validation techniques, data cleansing methods, and access control measures, businesses can ensure that integrated data is accurate, reliable, and secure.

Standardizing Frameworks for Seamless Interoperability

While integration tools provide technical solutions for connecting disparate data sources, achieving true interoperability requires industry-wide standardization. Standardized data formats, communication protocols, and governance frameworks ensure that different systems can exchange and interpret information consistently.

Several international standards have been developed to promote interoperability across various sectors:

Healthcare: The Health Level Seven (HL7) and Fast Healthcare Interoperability Resources (FHIR) frameworks allow different electronic health record systems to exchange patient data in a structured format, improving care coordination between hospitals, clinics, and insurance providers.

Finance: The ISO 20022 messaging standard enables seamless financial transactions by defining a common format for electronic data exchange between banks, payment processors, and regulatory institutions. Similarly, the Open Banking initiative mandates that banks provide standardized APIs to allow customers to securely share their financial data with third-party fintech applications.

Government & Public Sector: The National Information Exchange Model (NIEM) provides a structured framework for data sharing between government agencies, enabling better coordination in areas such as law enforcement, disaster response, and public health management.

Standardization is particularly crucial in industries dealing with sensitive data, where inconsistencies in data handling can lead to compliance violations, security breaches, and operational inefficiencies. For instance, global companies operating in multiple jurisdictions must comply with varying data protection regulations, such as the General Data Protection Regulation (GDPR) in Europe and the California Consumer Privacy Act (CCPA) in the United States. Implementing standardized frameworks ensures that businesses can navigate regulatory complexities while maintaining interoperability.

Despite the benefits of standardization, widespread adoption remains a challenge. Many organizations still rely on legacy systems that are incompatible with modern standards, requiring costly upgrades and manual data conversion processes. Additionally, some companies hesitate to embrace open standards due to concerns over data security, competitive advantage, and regulatory uncertainty.

To encourage broader adoption, governments, industry leaders, and technology providers must collaborate to establish clear guidelines, incentives, and support structures for organizations transitioning to standardized frameworks. Training programs, regulatory incentives, and cross-industry partnerships can facilitate smoother integration and drive long-term interoperability.

The Future of Data Integration in a Connected World

As technology advances, new innovations are shaping the future of data integration and interoperability. Emerging technologies such as artificial intelligence (AI), blockchain, and the Internet of Things

(IoT) are revolutionizing how organizations process and share information.

Artificial Intelligence & Machine Learning: AI-driven data integration tools can automate data mapping, anomaly detection, and predictive analytics, making it easier to merge structured and unstructured datasets from multiple sources. These technologies help organizations uncover hidden patterns, detect fraud, and optimize decision-making processes with minimal manual intervention.

Blockchain for Secure Data Sharing: Blockchain provides a decentralized, tamper-proof ledger that ensures the integrity and security of shared data. Industries such as supply chain management, healthcare, and finance are increasingly adopting blockchain to create transparent, auditable records that reduce fraud and improve trust among stakeholders.

Internet of Things (IoT) & Edge Computing: With billions of connected devices generating real-time data, interoperability between IoT systems is essential. Edge computing—which processes data closer to its source—reduces latency and enhances real-time decision-making, particularly in smart cities, autonomous vehicles, and industrial automation.

As cloud-based architectures, AI-driven automation, and decentralized data models continue to evolve, the future of data integration lies in intelligent, adaptive systems that can seamlessly communicate across industries, geographies, and technological ecosystems. Organizations that invest in interoperable frameworks, ethical data governance, and innovative integration technologies will be best positioned to thrive in an increasingly data-driven world.

By breaking down data silos, embracing standardized protocols, and leveraging emerging innovations, businesses can build bridges of connectivity that unlock new opportunities for collaboration, efficiency, and digital transformation. The future of data is not in isolated information but in its ability to flow freely, securely, and intelligently empowering organizations to create value, drive innovation, and build a truly interconnected global digital ecosystem.

CHAPTER NINE

ILLUMINATING THE STARS DATA VISUALIZATION AND COMMUNICATION

Data, a resource that drives strategic planning, innovation, and decision-making, is frequently referred to as the "new oil" in an era of digital transformation. However, data alone is meaningless unless it can be interpreted and communicated effectively. The sheer volume of information available today presents both opportunities and challenges. While organizations collect vast amounts of data, extracting meaningful insights from raw numbers requires a thoughtful approach to visualization and communication.

Data visualization is the art of transforming complex datasets into clear, insightful representations that allow audiences to grasp patterns, trends, and relationships at a glance. Unlike traditional reports filled with spreadsheets and text-heavy analysis, visual representations enable quicker comprehension and facilitate better decision-making. Charts, graphs, maps, and dashboards condense intricate data structures into digestible forms, making it easier for people to draw meaningful conclusions.

Consider the role of data visualization in public health. During the COVID-19 pandemic, real-time dashboards and heat maps provided governments, medical professionals, and the public with critical insights into infection rates, vaccination progress, and hospital capacity. Without such visual tools, policymakers would have struggled to allocate resources efficiently, and individuals might have been left without clear guidance on safety measures. Similarly, in climate science, global temperature maps and carbon emission charts serve as powerful visual narratives that highlight the urgency of environmental action. By presenting overwhelming scientific data in a clear, visually compelling manner, these tools help governments, organizations, and activists rally support sustainability initiatives.

The impact of data visualization extends to corporate decision-making as well. Businesses rely on interactive dashboards to track financial performance, customer behavior, and operational efficiency. Instead of sifting through endless spreadsheets, executives can make data-driven decisions using key performance indicators (KPIs) displayed in real time. For instance, an e-commerce company might use sales heat maps to identify geographic regions with high customer demand, allowing them to optimize marketing efforts and supply chain logistics.

Even in journalism and media, data visualization has transformed storytelling. Election coverage, for example, often features real-time electoral maps that update as votes are counted. Without these interactive tools, audiences would struggle to follow the progress of elections or understand regional voting patterns. Similarly, investigative journalists use data-driven graphics to expose corruption, economic disparities, and social trends, making complex stories more accessible to the public.

However, with great power comes great responsibility. Misleading visualizations—whether intentional or accidental—can distort reality and misinform audiences. Manipulating axes, using misleading scales, or cherry-picking data points can create false narratives that skew public perception. Ethical data visualization requires transparency, accuracy, and an understanding of cognitive biases that might influence interpretation.

Designing Impactful Visualizations: Principles and Techniques

Creating an effective data visualization is both a science and an art. It requires a deep understanding of human cognition, design principles, and the specific goals of the visualization. Poorly designed charts can confuse or mislead, while well-crafted ones can reveal insights that might otherwise remain hidden.

The first step in designing a visualization is selecting the right format for the data. Different types of data require different visualization techniques:

Line graphs are best for tracking trends over time, such as stock prices or temperature changes.

Bar charts are ideal for comparing categorical data, such as sales performance by region.

Pie charts (though often overused) work best for showing proportions, such as market share distribution.

Scatter plots reveal correlations between variables, such as the relationship between income levels and education.

Heat maps highlight patterns across large datasets, such as crime rates in different neighborhoods.

Choosing the wrong visualization format can lead to confusion. For example, using a pie chart to compare more than five categories can make it difficult for viewers to discern differences. Similarly, presenting time-series data in a bar chart instead of a line graph can obscure trends and mislead the audience.

Color theory plays a crucial role in visualization. Effective use of color can highlight key insights, draw attention to trends, and differentiate categories. However, poor color choices can result in confusion or even accessibility issues. For instance, relying on red and green in financial reports can be problematic for individuals with color blindness. Instead, using colorblind-friendly palettes ensures that visualizations remain inclusive and effective.

Simplification and clarity are essential in data visualization. A common mistake is overloading charts with excessive labels, gridlines, or decorative elements that do not add value. Cluttered visualizations make it difficult for viewers to extract meaningful insights. A well-designed chart should focus on the most important data points and use whitespace effectively to enhance readability.

Interactivity has become an increasingly important feature in modern data visualization. Tools like Tableau, Power BI, and D3.js allow users to explore datasets dynamically, filter information based on their needs, and drill down into specifics. Interactive dashboards provide flexibility, making it easier for decision-makers to extract customized insights rather than relying on static charts. Psychology also plays a role in how data is perceived. People have cognitive biases that affect interpretation, such as the anchoring effect (relying too heavily on the first piece of information presented) or the framing effect (where data presentation influences decision-making). Understanding these biases helps visualization designers create clearer and more honest representations.

Communicating Insights Effectively:

The Human Element in Data Interpretation

While data visualization is a powerful tool, effective communication ensures that insights are understood and acted upon. The most well-designed chart is meaningless if the audience cannot grasp its significance. Communication bridges the gap between raw data and informed decision-making.

One of the most important aspects of data communication is storytelling. Data should not be presented in isolation; instead, it should be framed within a compelling narrative that gives context and meaning. For example, a simple line graph showing an increase in homelessness might be impactful, but when paired with stories of individuals affected by the crisis, it becomes a powerful call to action.

Tailoring communication to the audience is also critical. A data scientist presenting findings to a team of analysts might use technical language and statistical confidence intervals, whereas a business executive may need high-level summaries and actionable insights. A policymaker might require data framed in terms of societal impact, while the general public may respond best to relatable, real-world examples.

The role of social media in data communication has also grown. Platforms like Twitter, LinkedIn, and Instagram have popularized micro-visualizations—short, engaging data snippets that convey insights quickly. Infographics, animated charts, and interactive web-based tools make data more accessible and shareable. However, this trend has also led to the spread of misinformation, where misleading charts or out-of-context statistics go viral, shaping public opinion in unintended ways.

The future of data visualization and communication is increasingly immersive. Technologies such as augmented reality (AR) and virtual reality (VR) allow users to explore data in three-dimensional spaces, providing new perspectives on complex datasets. AI-driven natural language processing (NLP) enabling more intuitive interactions with data, allowing users to ask questions and receive visual responses in real time.

In an interconnected world where data influences everything from finance and healthcare to politics and education, mastering data visualization and communication is more important than ever. Those who can distill vast amounts of information into clear, compelling narratives will shape the future—illuminating the stars of information in a galaxy of complexity. By combining analytical rigor with creative storytelling, we can ensure that data is not just seen but understood, trusted, and used to drive meaningful change.

CHAPTER TEN

THE FUTURE OF THE DATAVERSE TRENDS AND TRANSFORMATIONS

The world is experiencing an unprecedented explosion of data. Every second, vast amounts of information are generated from social media interactions, financial transactions, scientific research, healthcare systems, IoT devices, and beyond. The digital age has transformed data into the backbone of modern civilization, influencing industries, economies, and societies on a scale never seen before.

As the Dataverse continues to expand, new trends and technological advancements are shaping the way information is collected, stored, processed, and utilized. The rapid growth of artificial intelligence (AI), cloud computing, blockchain, and quantum computing is revolutionizing the way we interact with data. These transformations not only bring efficiency and innovation but also raise critical concerns about ethics, security, privacy, and regulation.

Understanding the future of the Dataverse requires an in-depth exploration of emerging technologies, the evolution of data analytics, and the shifting paradigms in governance and security. The ability to harness and manage this vast and ever-growing pool of data will define the competitive edge of businesses, the efficiency of governments, and the well-being of societies.

The Rise of AI and Automation in Data Processing

Artificial intelligence is at the forefront of data evolution, enabling machines to process and analyze vast datasets faster and more accurately than ever before. Machine learning algorithms, deep learning frameworks, and natural language processing (NLP) techniques are reshaping industries by extracting insights from structured and unstructured data.

In healthcare, AI-driven data analytics is transforming patient care by enabling early disease detection, personalized treatment plans, and predictive modeling for outbreaks. In finance, AI-powered fraud detection systems analyze transaction patterns in real time, identifying anomalies and preventing financial crimes. In marketing, AI analyzes consumer behavior, predicts trends, and automates personalized recommendations, enhancing customer engagement and business outcomes.

The increasing role of automation in data processing is also changing traditional workflows. Robotic Process Automation (RPA) is being deployed across industries to automate repetitive tasks such as data entry, extraction, and reporting. AI-driven data governance systems ensure compliance with regulatory requirements by continuously monitoring and classifying sensitive information.

While AI and automation improve efficiency, they also introduce challenges. The reliance on algorithms for decision-making raises ethical concerns about bias, fairness, and transparency. The "black box" nature of some AI models makes it difficult to explain how decisions are made, leading to potential risks in critical applications such as hiring, law enforcement, and credit scoring. Addressing these concerns requires advancements in explainable AI, ethical AI frameworks, and human oversight mechanisms.

Edge Computing and the Decentralization of Data

The traditional model of centralized data processing in cloud environments is being challenged by the rise of edge computing. As billions of connected devices generate data at unprecedented rates, real-time processing and low-latency responses have become critical. Edge computing brings computation closer to the data source, reducing the need to transfer massive datasets to distant data centers.

Industries such as autonomous vehicles, smart cities, and industrial automation are increasingly adopting edge computing to enhance efficiency and responsiveness. Self-driving cars, for example, rely on real-time processing of sensor data to make split-second decisions without relying on distant cloud servers. Smart cities use edge computing for traffic management, public safety, and environmental monitoring, optimizing resources and improving urban living conditions.

The decentralization of data processing also enhances security and privacy. By processing sensitive data locally, organizations can reduce exposure to cyber threats and ensure compliance with stringent data protection regulations. However, managing distributed data infrastructure presents new challenges, including interoperability, scalability, and governance. The future of the Dataverse will require robust frameworks that balance the benefits of edge computing with the need for centralized control and standardization.

The Evolution of Data Storage: From Cloud to Quantum Computing

The demand for data storage is growing exponentially, pushing traditional storage technologies to their limits. Cloud computing has become the dominant model for storing and accessing data, offering scalability, cost-effectiveness, and flexibility. However, as data volumes continue to rise, new storage paradigms are emerging to address performance and efficiency challenges.

Quantum computing is poised to revolutionize data storage and processing by leveraging the principles of quantum mechanics. Unlike classical computing, which relies on binary bits (0s and 1s), quantum computing uses quantum bits (qubits) that can exist in multiple states simultaneously. This allows quantum computers to perform complex calculations at speeds unattainable by traditional systems.

The implications of quantum computing for the Dataverse are profound. Advanced quantum algorithms could drastically enhance cryptographic security, making current encryption methods obsolete. Quantum-powered machine learning models could unlock new frontiers in data analytics, solving problems that are currently infeasible for classical computers. However, widespread adoption of quantum computing remains in its early stages, requiring further advancements in hardware, software, and algorithm development.

The Integration of Blockchain in Data Security and Integrity

As data breaches and cyber threats continue to rise, organizations are seeking innovative solutions to enhance data security and integrity. Blockchain technology, originally developed for cryptocurrencies, is emerging as a powerful tool for secure and transparent data management.

Blockchain enables decentralized and tamper-proof record-keeping, ensuring data integrity and reducing the risk of fraud. Industries such as healthcare, finance, and supply chain management are exploring blockchain for secure transactions, identity verification, and provenance tracking. In healthcare, blockchain can provide a secure framework for patient records, ensuring privacy while enabling interoperability across medical institutions. In finance, decentralized ledgers can enhance transparency in transactions, reducing the risk of fraud and improving regulatory compliance.

Despite its advantages, blockchain adoption faces challenges such as scalability, energy consumption, and regulatory uncertainty. The future of blockchain in the Dataverse will depend on advancements in efficiency, governance frameworks, and integration with existing data infrastructures.

Ethical Data Governance and Global Regulations

As data becomes a critical asset, ethical considerations and regulatory frameworks are playing an increasingly important role in shaping the future of the Dataverse. Governments and organizations are under pressure to ensure data privacy, prevent misuse, and establish transparent governance mechanisms.

The introduction of regulations such as the General Data Protection Regulation (GDPR) in Europe and the California Consumer Privacy Act (CCPA) in the U.S. reflects the growing emphasis on data rights and accountability. These laws impose strict guidelines on how personal data is collected, processed, and shared, giving individuals greater control over their information.

The rise of AI-driven data analytics and surveillance technologies has sparked debates about digital ethics and human rights. Concerns about mass data collection, facial recognition, and algorithmic bias have led to calls for stricter oversight and ethical AI development. Organizations are now required to adopt ethical data practices, ensuring transparency, fairness, and accountability in data-driven decision-making.

The future of data governance will likely see the emergence of global regulatory standards, cross-border data-sharing agreements, and AI ethics councils to address the challenges of a hyper-connected world.

The Dawn of a Data-Driven Society

The future of the Dataverse is one of limitless potential and profound transformation. As data continues to shape industries, governments, and human interactions, embracing innovation while ensuring ethical responsibility will be key to navigating the evolving digital landscape.

AI, edge computing, quantum computing, blockchain, and data governance are not just technological trends—they are foundational shifts that will redefine how we generate, store, analyze, and secure information. The organizations and individuals who can adapt to these changes, harness the power of data responsibly, and leverage emerging technologies will lead the way in the data-driven future.

The Dataverse is no longer just a concept; it is the reality we live in. How we navigate its complexities, harness its potential, and address its challenges will determine the course of human progress in the decades to come. The future is data-driven, and those who master the Dataverse will shape the world of tomorrow.

Embracing the Data Revolution

As we stand at the crossroads of a digital revolution, the Dataverse has become the fabric that weaves together industries, societies, and human experiences. The rapid proliferation of data, fueled by technological advancements in artificial intelligence, quantum computing, blockchain, and edge computing, is reshaping the way we live, work, and interact with the world. From real-time analytics that drive business decisions to predictive models that revolutionize healthcare, data is no longer just an asset—it is the foundation upon which the future is being built.

However, with great power comes great responsibility. The evolution of the Dataverse presents both unparalleled opportunities and complex challenges. While the potential for innovation is limitless, concerns surrounding data privacy, security, ethics, and governance must be addressed to ensure a sustainable and equitable digital future.

As we navigate this vast and ever-expanding Dataverse, the key to success lies in our ability to harness data responsibly, adapt to emerging technologies, and create a framework for ethical and secure data management. The future is not just about data collection and analysis, it is about understanding, interpreting, and applying data in ways that enhance human lives while mitigating risks.

Balancing Innovation with Ethics

One of the most pressing concerns in the Dataverse is the ethical use of data. The widespread adoption of artificial intelligence and machine learning has brought about incredible efficiencies, but it has also exposed biases, misinformation, and ethical dilemmas. Facial recognition technologies, algorithm-driven decision-making, and mass surveillance have sparked global debates about digital rights and privacy.

Regulatory bodies and organizations must work together to create ethical frameworks that promote fairness, transparency, and accountability in data-driven decision-making. Striking the right balance between innovation and ethical responsibility will be crucial in ensuring that data serves humanity rather than exploits it. The rise of ethical AI principles, responsible data governance models, and privacy-enhancing technologies will play a vital role in shaping the future of the Dataverse.

The Human Element in a Data-Driven World

Amidst the algorithms and automation, one undeniable truth remains—data is only as valuable as the human insights derived from it. The human mind, with its creativity, intuition, and critical thinking, remains an irreplaceable force in the Dataverse. While AI and automation can process vast amounts of data at lightning speeds, human expertise is required to interpret results, ask the right questions, and make ethical judgments.

As we advance into a data-centric future, the role of data literacy will become more critical than ever. Individuals, businesses, and governments must cultivate data literacy skills to effectively navigate the complexities of the Dataverse. Understanding how to read, analyze, and question data will empower individuals to make informed decisions and prevent the misuse of information.

Furthermore, the importance of interdisciplinary collaboration cannot be overstated. The Dataverse is not just for data scientists and technologists—it is for policymakers, business leaders, healthcare professionals, educators, and everyday citizens. Bridging the gap between technical expertise and domain knowledge will ensure that data-driven solutions address real-world problems with precision and impact.

The Future is Collaborative and Decentralized

The future of the Dataverse will be shaped by collaboration. The era of siloed data management is giving way to a more interconnected and decentralized approach. Governments, organizations, and research institutions are working toward open data ecosystems that foster innovation while maintaining security and compliance.

Blockchain technology and decentralized data networks are paving the way for more transparent and secure data-sharing mechanisms. The idea of "data ownership" is shifting, with individuals gaining greater control over their personal information through self-sovereign identity systems and encrypted digital wallets. As the Dataverse evolves, the emphasis will be on creating trusted networks where data can be shared responsibly, benefiting all stakeholders while minimizing risks.

In addition, cross-border data governance will play a crucial role in shaping global data policies. As data knows no geographical boundaries, international cooperation will be necessary to establish standardized frameworks for data protection, cybersecurity, and ethical AI development. Governments must work together to prevent data monopolies, ensure equitable access to digital resources, and uphold the principles of a free and open internet.

A Data-Driven Tomorrow

The Dataverse is not a distant concept, it is the reality we are living in today. Every click, every transaction, and every sensor reading contributes to an ever-growing digital landscape that influences every aspect of our lives. The choices we make today will determine the trajectory of the Dataverse for generations to come.

Will we use data to solve the world's most pressing challenges, from climate change to global health crises? Will we create a future where data is a force for good, empowering individuals and communities rather than exploiting them? Or will we allow unchecked technological advancements to lead us into a world of surveillance, inequality, and ethical dilemmas?

The answers to these questions lie in the hands of data scientists, policymakers, innovators, and everyday citizens. By fostering a culture of ethical data use, investing in education and digital literacy, and promoting collaboration across industries and nations, we can build a future where data serves as a tool for progress, not division.

As we continue our journey through the Dataverse, one thing is clear—the road ahead is filled with possibility. The key to navigating this evolving landscape is not just in the technology we create but in the values we uphold. A data-driven world must also be a **h**uman-centered world, where innovation, ethics, and inclusivity go hand in hand.

The Dataverse is vast, dynamic, and ever-changing. The question is: how will we navigate it? The answer lies in our ability to harness the power of data wisely, ethically, and collaboratively ensuring that the future we build is one of progress, knowledge, and share prosperity.